D1601326

THE HACKER'S DICTIONARY

The Hacker's Dictionary

A Guide to the World of Computer Wizards

GUY L. STEELE JR.

DONALD R. WOODS

RAPHAEL A. FINKEL

MARK R. CRISPIN

RICHARD M. STALLMAN

GEOFFREY S. GOODFELLOW

HARPER & ROW, PUBLISHERS, New York
Cambridge, Philadelphia, San Francisco, London
Mexico City, São Paulo, Sydney

1817

"Ada" is a registered trademark of the U.S. Government–Ada Joint Program Office. "ADM" is a trademark and "Dumb Terminal" is a registered trademark of Lear Siegler, Inc. "Apple" is a registered trademark of Apple Computer, Inc. "Coca-Cola" and "Coke" are registered trademarks of the Coca-Cola Company. "DEC," "DECSYSTEM-20," "DEC tape," "PDP," "VAX," "VMS," and "VT" are trademarks of Digital Equipment Corporation. "IBM" and "Selectric" are registered trademarks of International Business Machines Corporation. "Kleenex" is a registered trademark of Kimberly-Clark Corporation. "Multics" is a registered trademark of Honeywell Inc. "Pepsi" is a registered trademark of Pepsico, Inc. "Radio Shack" and "TRS-80" are registered trademarks of Tandy Corporation. "Star Trek" is a registered trademark of Paramount Pictures Corporation. "Teletype" is a registered trademark of Teletype Corporation. "TENEX" is a registered trademark of Bolt Beranek and Newman Inc. "UNIX" is a trademark of Bell Laboratories.

THE HACKER'S DICTIONARY. Copyright © 1983 by Guy L. Steele Jr. All rights reserved. Printed in the United States of America. No part of this book may be used or reproduced in any manner whatsoever without written permission except in the case of brief quotations embodied in critical articles and reviews. For information address Harper & Row, Publishers, Inc., 10 East 53rd Street, New York, N.Y. 10022. Published simultaneously in Canada by Fitzhenry & Whiteside Limited, Toronto.

FIRST EDITION

Designer: Sidney Feinberg

Library of Congress Cataloging in Publication Data
Main entry under title:

The Hacker's dictionary.

(Colophon books; 1082)

1. Electronic data processing—Terminology—Anecdotes, facetiae, satire, etc. I. Steele, Guy.
PN6231.E4H3 1983   001.64'014   83-47573
ISBN 0-06-091082-8 (pbk.)

83 84 85 86 87 10 9 8 7 6 5 4 3 2 1

Contents

The Menu

There are many dictionaries of computer buzzwords and jargon. This book is different. It is a dictionary of slang.

Jargon consists of technical words that are needed for very precise communication in a specialized subject. Economists, truck drivers, chemists, and steelworkers all use a specialized vocabulary to convey technical meanings.

Slang, on the other hand, is used for fun, for *human* communication rather than technical communication. Slang is often derived from jargon. When a bit of technical jargon is used in an extended or metaphorical way, it becomes slang.

Many "computer" words are making their way into everyday use. Thanks to the proliferation of home computers, many people have heard of bytes, RAM, memory banks, terminals, processors, and floppy disks.

You won't find those words defined here. This, we warn you, is supposed to be a *fun* book.

These are the words used for fun by the people who use computers for fun: the hackers. Here you will find almost nothing of those awful computer languages such as BASIC that can be written but not spoken. This book is, in fact, a revised version of the famous "jargon file,"[1] a dictionary of slang terms cooperatively maintained by hackers at advanced computer laboratories at Stanford University, the Massachusetts Institute of Technology (MIT), Carnegie-Mellon University (CMU), and other places such as Yale University, Princeton University, and Worcester Polytechnic Institute (WPI). Some of these words are fairly new; others have been used for over two decades. Some arose in the computer laboratory; others were borrowed from other fields.

Our gang of six contributed to this file over the years, and to this revision for publication. (Steele coordinated the effort and did

---

1. It should have been called "slang file," but it wasn't, and it recently has been referred to in the media by the name "jargon file," so now we are stuck with it.

most of the polish work. Occasional first-person references in the main text are his unless otherwise identified.) Many other hackers around the country, too numerous to list, made helpful suggestions; to them we are grateful. For this edition, pronunciation keys have been added for all those words that are not ordinary English words, and many cross-references, examples, and explanatory notes have been added. We have tried to keep technical details to a minimum. A word is included only if it is amusing or unusual, or if it peculiarly illuminates some aspect of hacker culture.

We hope you enjoy this book.

Confessions of a Happy Hacker

by Guy Steele

I was a teen-age hacker.

When I was about twelve or so, a lab secretary at MIT who knew I was "interested in science" (it might be more accurate to say "a latent nerd") arranged for one of the computer hackers there to give me an informal tour. I remember stumbling around racks full of circuit boards and wires, a screeching cabinet that printed a full page every six seconds, and rows of blinking lights: the computer room was crammed full of equipment with no obvious organization. One set of gray cabinets had some trophies and plaques sitting on it: this was the PDP-6 computer that, running a program called MacHack, consistently won prizes by outwitting human players in chess tournaments. This PDP-6 was also versatile: it had two speakers and a stereo amplifier sitting on top of it. The hacker typed a couple of commands on a keyboard, and the PDP-6 burst into a Bach Brandenburg Concerto (no. 6, as I recall).

One part of that tour stands out most clearly in my mind. I was told to sit down in front of a large, round, glass screen, and given a box that had some buttons and a stick on the top. My hacker guide typed a command on the keyboard, and suddenly, green and purple space ships appeared on the screen! The purple one started shooting little red dots at the green one, which was soon obliterated in a multicolored shower of sparkles. The green ship was "mine," and the hacker had expertly shot it down. This was a color version of Space War, one of the very first video games.

Remember that this was years before "Apple" and "TRS-80" had become household words. Back then computers were still rather mysterious, hidden away in giant corporations and university laboratories.

Playing Space War was fun, but I learned nothing of programming then. I had the true fascination of computers revealed to me in November, 1968, when a chum slipped me the news that our school (Boston Latin School, of Boston, Massachusetts) had an IBM computer locked up in the basement. I was dubious. I had earlier narrowly avoided buying from a senior a ticket to the fourth-floor swimming pool (Boston Latin has only three stories, and no swimming pool at all), and assumed this was another scam. So of course I laughed in his face.

When he persisted, I checked it out. Sure enough, in a locked basement room was an IBM 1130 computer. If you want all the specs: 4096 words of memory, 16 bits per word, a 15-character-per-second Selectric ("golf ball") printer, and a card reader (model 1442) that could read 300 cards per minute. Yes, this was back in the days of punched cards. Personal computers were completely unheard-of then.

Nominally the computer was for the training of juniors and seniors, but I cajoled a math teacher into lending me a computer manual and spent all of Thanksgiving vacation reading it.

I was hooked.

No doubt about it. I was born to be a hacker. Fortunately, I didn't let my studies suffer (as many young hackers do), but every spare moment I thought about the computer. It was spellbinding. I wanted to know all about it: what it could and couldn't do, how its programs worked, what its circuits looked like. During study halls, lunch, and after school, I could be found in the computer room, punching programs onto cards and running them through the computer.

I was not the only one. Very soon there was a small community of IBM 1130 hackers. We helped to maintain the computer and we tutored our less fanatical fellow students in the ways of computing. What could possibly compensate us for these chores? Free rein in the computer room.

Soon after that, I developed into one of the unauthorized but tolerated "random people" hanging around the MIT Artificial Intelligence Laboratory. A random hacker is to a computer laboratory much as a groupie is to a rock band: not really doing useful work, but emotionally involved and contributing to the *ambiance,* if nothing else. After a while, I was haunting the computer rooms at off-hours, talking to people but more often looking for chances to run programs. Sometimes "randoms" such as I were quite help-ful, operating the computers for no pay and giving advice to col-lege students who were having trouble. Sometimes, however, we were quite a nuisance. Once, I was ejected from the Artificial Intelligence Laboratory by none other than Richard Greenblatt, the very famous hacker who wrote the MacHack program with which the PDP-6 had won its chess trophies. He threw me out because I was monopolizing the one terminal that produced let-ter-quality copy. (I was using the computer to write "personal-ized" form letters to various computer manufacturers, asking for machine manuals.) I deserved to be tossed out, and gave him no argument. But when you're hooked, you're hooked, and I was undaunted: within a week or two I was back again.

Eventually I got a part-time job as a programmer at MIT's Pro-ject MAC computer laboratory. There I became a full-fledged member of the hacker community, and ultimately an MIT gradu-ate student.

I was never a lone hacker, but one of many. Despite stories you may have read about anti-social nerds glued permanently to dis-play screens, totally addicted to the computer, hackers have (human) friends too. Often these friendships are formed and main-tained through the computer.

At one time, the MIT Artificial Intelligence Laboratory had one common telephone number, extension 6765, and a public-address system. The phone was answered "six-seven-six-five," or some-times "Fibonacci of twenty," since, as mathematicians know, 6765 is the twentieth Fibonacci number. Through this number and the public-address system, it was easy to call and reach anyone and everyone. In particular, one could easily ask, "Who wants to go for Chinese food?" and get ten or fifteen people for an expedition.

"Unfortunately," says MIT hacker Richard Stallman, "most of the people and terminals have moved to other floors, where the 6765 number does not reach. The ninth floor, the lab's ancient heart, is becoming totally filled with machines, leaving no room for people, who must move to other floors. Now I can't even call up and find out if anyone is hungry."

Stallman can, however, still call us all up using the computer. Through timesharing (where many people use one computer) and networking (where many computers are connected together), the computer makes possible a new form of human communication, better than the telephone and the postal system put together. You can send a message by electronic mail and get a reply within two minutes, or you can just link two terminals together and have a conversation.

MIT has no monopoly on hackers. In the 1960s and 1970s hackers congregated around any computer center that made computer time available for "play." (Some of this play turned out to be very important work, but hacking is done mostly for fun, for its own sake, for the pure joy of it.) Because universities tend to be more flexible than corporations in this regard, most hackers' dens arose in university laboratories. While some of these hackers were unauthorized "random people" like me, many hackers were paid employees who chose to stay after hours and work on their own projects—or even continue their usual work—purely for pleasure.

The hacker community became still larger and more closely knit in the early 1970s, when the government funded a project to see whether it would be useful to let the computers at dozens of universities and other sites "talk" to each other. The project succeeded and produced the famous ARPANET, a network that now links hundreds of computers across the country. Through the ARPANET, researchers can share programs, trade research results, and send electronic mail—both to individuals and to massive mailing lists. Best of all, it allowed once-isolated hackers to talk to each other via computer.

The result is a nation-wide hackers' community, now one decade old. In some ways the community serves as a geographically dispersed think tank. When Rubik's Cube became popular, one hacker created an electronic mailing list of "Cube hackers." (Such mailing lists are routinely created for new topics of interest.) The network buzzed, and continues to buzz, with expositions of some very deep mathematics in efforts to solve various puzzles about the Cube. What, for example, is the smallest number of twists required to solve the Cube? This question is still unanswered; but some progress has been made, and hackers across the country continue to discuss and to fret over its solution via computer.

Hackers do more than talk, however; they *hack*. Although no two people are alike, there are certain traits that are typical of hackers.

The cardinal qualification is that hackers like to use computers. The word CYCLE, as used by hackers, refers to the fundamental unit of work done by a computer, so we say that hackers crave cycles. The more cycles available, the more a hacker gets out of the computer.

As a direct result of this craving, a hacker will frequently wake up at dinner time and go to bed after breakfast, or perhaps get up at noon and sack out at 4:00 A.M. (See the terms PHASE and NIGHT MODE for more information on hackers' sleeping schedules.) Hackers do this because the computer has its own circadian rhythms to which hackers willingly adjust themselves. These rhythms in turn grow out of the heavier demands for the computer during the day than at night. Hackers will therefore work late into the evening or night, when other computer users aren't competing for cycles. It's more fun, after all, to use the computer when it's responding at split-second speeds.

Most such hackers are single. Hackers do get married, but the responsibilities of family life don't always mix well with typical hacker life style. When I was at MIT, I would sometimes work nights for a month at a time. Now that I am married, I find that I can hack only in spurts, one or two days a week. This book, by the way, is a hack of sorts. The manuscript was prepared using a computer, and nearly all of the work was done after midnight.

The truly dedicated hacker does little else but eat, sleep, and hack. Of these activities, eating is the only social activity, so rather than eat at home alone, a hacker will usually go out to eat with his hacker friends. While hackers may sleep according to different schedules, most arrange to be awake and at the laboratory around 6:00 P.M., at which time one or more dinner expeditions usually head out.

For some reason, Chinese food is particularly favored by most hackers. You will find several references to Chinese Szechuan and Hunan cuisine in this dictionary. Other spicy cuisines, such as Mexican and Indian, are also enjoyed by hackers, but Chinese is the definite favorite.

Many shorthand expressions have developed for discussing food and local restaurants. At MIT one might hear: "Foodp?"; "Smallp?"; "T."; "T!" Translated, this means roughly:

"Do you want to eat now?"
"Maybe; what would you think of going to Joyce Chen's Small Eating Place?"
"Okay by me."
"Then I'll join you!"

When you walk up to the terminal of a time-shared computer, the first thing you must do is to "log in," that is, tell the computer who you are. To do this, you type in your "computer i.d." or "login name." Different computers have different ideas of what a login name should be. Some use numbers or other codes (see the entry for PPN), some use your last name, some use your initials. Many computers limit login names to either three or six characters, so full names or last names can't be used in general.

As a result everyone acquires a login name, which you need to know to communicate with another hacker via computer. A login name serves in much the same way as a CB "handle." I have friends whom I know only by login name; I have no idea what their real names are. Once, at a wedding, I ran into a good hacker friend who was also a guest there. I recalled his login name instantly, but was embarrassed that I couldn't immediately remember his real name in order to introduce him to a third person. It was SWAPPED OUT.

Login names are often used as nicknames, pronounced if possible and spelled if necessary. My wife and I met at MIT, and she still calls me "Gliss," because my login name was GLS. "Guy" sounds very weird to her. Some hackers (including Richard Stallman) actually prefer to be called by their login name.

Because the design and use of computers depend on other branches of science, a hacker has to have some knowledge of mathematics, physics, electronics, and other disciplines. Hackers typically have many other interests as well: science fiction, music, and chess are particularly popular.

The common theme, however, is the love of the computer. Hackers discuss science fiction through computerized mailing lists. A hacker is less likely to listen to music than to program a computer to play music. A hacker who can play only a middling game of chess can write a program that wins chess tournaments. Such are the compensations of a life at the keyboard.

Happy hacking!

A Hackish Note on How to Use This Book

BY RAPHAEL FINKEL AND DON WOODS

While hackers necessarily design and use unspeakable languages to control computers, they also have an unusual spoken language. Just as strange language had first attracted many of us to computers, we were struck by the queer vocabulary hackers would use to describe not only computer-related things but the wide world as well. Finkel decided to build a lexicon of the strange words and expressions that set this community apart, and the rest of us added to it over the years.

A lot of our slang can be figured out from context. Don Woods once told a waitress, "I think we're ready to go, MODULO paying the check." And there's the time he asked a flight attendant to "please SNARF me a magazine." Neither of them batted an eye. It is the most commonly used jargon words—the ones loaded with subtle connotations accumulated over the years—that are the hardest to define.

This book is arranged as a dictionary, and you may skip around reading individual definitions if you please. However, definitions occurring later in the book purposely build on earlier ones, and we think you will get more fun out of it if you read the book straight through in alphabetical order.

We want to warn the reader that not all the expressions you will find here are in common use. Many are regional; some are obsolete. Some are used every day, and others are heard only occasionally. To give you an idea, here is a list of our favorite and perhaps most frequently used words:

BAR	BOGOSITY	CRUFTY
BARF	BOGUS	FEATURE
BAZ	BUG	FLAME
BELLS AND WHISTLES	CANONICAL	FLAVOR

FLUSH	LOSER	PHASE OF THE MOON
FOO	MAGIC	RANDOM
FOOBAR	MOBY	THE REAL WORLD
FROB	MODULO	SNARF
HACK	MUMBLE	VANILLA
KLUDGE	PHASE	WIZARD

By and large, computer people have an enormous range of intellectual interests; you will see this fact reflected in the lexicon. While they use slang for fun, most computer people are highly literate, highly articulate, and sticklers for grammar. Don't expect to impress people by overusing the words you find here. They are the spice, not the bread and butter, of everyday conversation.

Grokking Hacker Grammar

For the most part, hackerese fits within the framework of ordinary English speech. There are a few rules, however, that are unusual in everyday English but are very commonly used in hackerese. (These extra rules of grammar reflect the fact that hackers enjoy playing with language. Most are quite aware of when they are breaking the rules of standard English.)

Verb Doubling

A standard construction in English is to double a verb and use it as an exclamation, such as "bang, bang!" or "quack, quack!" Most of these are names for noises. Hackers also double verbs as a concise, sometimes sarcastic, comment on what the implied subject does. Also, a doubled verb is often used to terminate a conversation—in the process, remarking on the current state of affairs or what the speaker intends to do next. Verbs frequently doubled include WIN, LOSE, HACK, FLAME, BARF, and CHOMP. Typical examples of usage:

"The disk heads just crashed. Lose, lose."
"Mostly he just talked about his latest crock. Flame, flame."
"I think I'll go fix that bug now. Hack, hack!"

Standard doublings with subtle connotations are listed individually in the lexicon.

Sound-alike Slang

In the manner of cockney rhyming slang, hackers will often make rhymes or puns in order to convert an ordinary word or phrase into something more interesting. It is particularly FLAVOR-FUL if the phrase is bent so as to include some other slang word; thus, the computer hobbyist magazine *Dr. Dobb's Journal* is almost always referred to among hackers as *Dr. Frob's Journal*.

Terms of this kind in fairly wide use include names for newspapers:

> Boston *Herald American* becomes *Horrid (or Harried) American.*
> Boston *Globe* becomes Boston *Glob.*
> San Francisco *Chronicle* becomes the *Crocknicle.*
> *New York Times* becomes *New York Slime.*

Other standard terms include:

> "For historical reasons" becomes "for hysterical raisins."
> "Margaret Jacks Hall" (a building at Stanford) becomes "Marginal Hacks Hall."
> "Government property—do not duplicate" (seen on keys at MIT) is usually quoted as "government duplicity—do not propagate."

The -P Convention

This rule is unique, used by no one but hackers. A word or phrase is turned into a yes/no question by appending the letter *P*, which is pronounced as a separate syllable when spoken. This rule is derived from a convention of the LISP programming language, where the letter *P* at the end of a name denotes a "predicate"—that is, a function that returns "true" or "false" as its result.

For example, the question "Foodp?" (pronounced "food'pee," with the voice rising as for any question) means "Do you want to eat now?" The question "Colleen's-p?" is more specific: "Do you want to go eat at Colleen's Chinese Cuisine (a favorite restaurant near MIT)?" "Lose-p?" means "Are you LOSING?" or "Is it LOSING?" And so on.

As a special case, the question "State-of-the-world-p?" means "What's going on?" or "What are you doing (or about to do)?" The -P convention is used for this even though it isn't a yes/no question. A typical answer might be "The SYSTEM just CRASHED" or "I'm about to GRONK OUT." If the responder is feeling silly or obstinate, however, he will insist on interpreting it as a yes/no

question after all, and respond with "Yes, the world has a state."
The -P convention is often applied to new words at the spur of
the moment. The best of these is a GOSPERISM (that is, invented
by R. William Gosper). When we were at a Chinese restaurant, he
wanted to know whether someone would like to share with him
a two-person-sized bowl of soup. His inquiry was "Split-p soup?"
and everyone instantly knew what he meant. (After all, split pea
soup was not on the menu).

Overgeneralization

Hackers love to take advantage of the inconsistencies of English
by extending a general rule to cases where it doesn't apply. Children routinely do this when they say "teached" for "taught" or
"He goed there" for "He went there." Hackers do this quite inten-
tionally for more complicated words. One example:

> "Generous" becomes "generosity."
> "Porous" becomes "porosity."
> "Curious" becomes "curiosity."

Therefore:

> "Mysterious" becomes "mysteriosity."
> "Obvious" becomes "obviosity."
> "Dubious" becomes "dubiosity."

Less clearly:

> "Bogus" becomes "bogosity."

And, perhaps:

> "Ferrous" becomes "ferocity"!

Other examples: winnitude, disgustitude, hackitude, hackifi-
cation.

Spoken Inarticulations

Words such as "mumble," "sigh," and "groan" are spoken in
places where their referent might more naturally be used. It has
been suggested that this usage derives from the impossibility of
representing such noises in conversation by computer (see COM

MODE); one gets so used to typing "Sigh!" to indicate a sigh that one soon develops the vocal habit of saying the word instead of actually sighing. Another expression sometimes heard is "complain!" (meaning not "You, complain!" but "I have a complaint!").

How to Make Hacker Noises

Many of the words in this dictionary are ordinary English words that have acquired new meanings. Some appear to be English words but are pronounced differently, and many are new words. To keep things simple, we have included pronunciations only in the unusual cases. If no pronunciation is given for a word, it should be pronounced as an ordinary English word.

Also for simplicity, we do not use the complicated alphabets and pronunciation marks used in most dictionaries. These alphabets, such as the International Phonetic Alphabet, allow a very precise description of pronunciation but are hard to read if you're not familiar with them. We use the following simplified system: Syllables are separated by hyphens, except that an apostrophe follows an accented syllable. Consonants are pronounced as they usually are in English. The letter g is always hard, as in "got" rather than "giant"; ch is always soft, as in "child" rather than "chemist." The letter s is always as in "pass," and never a z sound as in "has"; but to prevent confusion, ss is sometimes used at the end of a syllable to emphasize this. Other consonants are also occasionally doubled for the same reason. The letter j always contains the leading d sound as used twice in "judge." Vowel sounds are represented as shown in the following table:

a	back, that
ay	bake, rain
ah	cot, father
aw	flaw, caught
e	less, men
ee	easy, ski
i	trip, hit
ie	life, sky
ow	out, how
oh	flow, sew
oy	boy, coin

uh	but, some
u	put, foot
oo	loot, through
y	yet
yoo	few

A colon—":"—is used for the "schwa" sound that is often written as an upside-down *e*. For example, the pronunciation of "kitten" would be *kit':n*, and of "magical" would be *maj'i-k:l*.

Some Overflow PDL

Various abbreviations are used throughout these definitions. Most refer to computer hardware and software. For example, one of the favorite computer languages in our hacker community is LISP. The two poles of the hacker's network that compiled this dictionary are the artificial intelligence laboratories at Stanford and MIT, and LISP has always been one language of choice for artificial intelligence research. A particular computer, the Digital Equipment Corporation (DEC) PDP-6, and its successors (the PDP-10 and DECSYSTEM-20) have until recently been the computers of choice for running LISP. The consequence is that technical words from the LISP language and the PDP-10 computer will occasionally appear in this dictionary. The EMACS text editor, also referred to, was one of the first "display editors" to be widely distributed. It is used as a standard against which new text editors for personal computers are measured. We have tried to keep such words to a minimum throughout.

THE HACKER'S DICTIONARY

AOS *(owss* [East coast], *ay'ahss* [West coast]*) verb.*
1. To add one to a number. Example: "Every time the computer finds a bad file it aoses the bad-file counter."
2. More generally, to increase the amount of something. Example: "Aos the campfire" means "Add more wood to the campfire." *Silly.*

Antonym: SOS.

This word is the name of a PDP-10 instruction that takes any memory location in the computer and adds one to it. AOS means "Add One and do not Skip." Why, you may ask, does the *S* stand for "Do not Skip" rather than for "Skip"? Ah, here is a beloved piece of PDP-10 folklore. There are eight such instructions: AOSE adds One and then Skips the next instruction if the result is Equal to zero; AOSG adds One and then Skips if the result is Greater than zero; AOSN adds One and then Skips if the result is Not zero; AOSA adds One and then Skips Always; and so on. Just plain AOS doesn't say when to skip, so it never skips. For similar reasons, AOJ means "Add One and do not Jump." Even more bizarre, SKIP means "Do not SKIP"! If you want to skip the next instruction, you must say "SKIPA." Likewise, JUMP means "Do not JUMP."

ARG *(ahrg) noun.*
An argument, in the mathematical sense only: a quantity accepted by a function or procedure. Example: "The sine function takes one arg, but the arc-tangent function can take either one or two args."

This is an abbreviation that has become a new word in its own right, just as "telephone" and "pianoforte" have become "phone" and "piano." Arguments to mathematical functions and computational procedures are discussed so frequently by hackers that this abbreviation saves a lot of time.

AUTOMAGICALLY *(aw'toh-maj'i-k:l-lee, aw'toh-maj'i-klee) adverb.*
Automatically, but in a way which, for some reason (typically because it is too complicated, or too ugly, or perhaps even too trivial), the speaker doesn't feel like explaining. Example: "Files that have a name ending in 'TMP' are automagically deleted when you log out." (This means "When you say goodbye to the computer, files with names ending in 'TMP' are deleted. How this happens is complicated and I don't want to get into it just now. Trust me, it works.")
See MAGIC.

BAGBITER *(bag'bie-t:r) noun.*
1. Something, such as a program or a computer, that fails to work or that works in a remarkably clumsy manner. Example: "This text editor won't let me make a file with a line longer than eighty characters! What a bagbiter!"
2. A person who has caused you some trouble, inadvertently or otherwise, typically by failing to program the computer properly.
   Synonyms: LOSER, CRETIN, CHOMPER.
   BAGBITING *adjective.* Having the quality of a bagbiter. "This bagbiting system won't let me compute the greatest common divisor of two negative numbers."
   Synonyms: LOSING, CRETINOUS, BLETCHEROUS, BARFUCIOUS, CHOMPING.
   BITE THE BAG *verb.* To fail in some manner. Example: "The computer keeps CRASHING every five minutes." "Yes, the disk controller is really biting the bag."
   The original meaning of this term was almost undoubtedly obscene, probably referring to the scrotum. In its current usage it has become almost completely sanitized.

BANG *noun.*
The character "!" (exclamation point).
   Synonyms: EXCL, SHRIEK. See CHARACTERS.
   This term is more popular at CMU than at MIT or Stanford. It is used to describe the character "!" itself rather than to

replace it. For example, one would not say, "Congratulations bang." On the other hand, if I wanted you to write "FOO!"—those exact four characters, on a piece of paper—I would tell you, "Write eff, oh, oh, bang."

BAR
The second metasyntactic variable, after FOO. If a hacker needs to invent exactly two names for things, he almost always picks the names "foo" and "bar." Example: "Suppose we have two functions, say, foo and bar. Now suppose foo calls bar . . ." See FOO, FOOBAR.

BARF
1. *interjection.* Term of disgust or frustration. See BLETCH.
2. *verb.* To say "Barf!" or a similar term of disgust (because one is annoyed or offended).
3. To fail to work because of unacceptable input; sometimes, to print an error message. Examples: "The division operation barfs if you try to divide by zero." (Division by zero fails in some unspecified spectacular way.) "The text editor barfs if you try to read in a new file before writing out the old one."
    BARFULOUS, BARFUCIOUS *adjective.* So ugly or offensive as to make someone barf.
    These meanings are derived from the common slang meaning of "barf," namely, "to vomit."

BAZ *(baz)*
1. The third metasyntactic variable, after FOO and BAR.
2. *interjection.* Term of mild annoyance. In this usage the pronunciation is often drawn out for two or three seconds, sometimes sounding like the bleating of a sheep: "Baaaaaaaaaz!"

BELLS AND WHISTLES *noun.*
Unnecessary (but often useful, convenient, or amusing) features of a program or other object. Example: "Now that we've got the basic program working, let's go back and add some bells and whistles."

On an automobile, things like power windows and quadraphonic sound would be bells and whistles.

This term is widely used, and not just in the hacker community. To understand it, think of a plain box that does a job well but is awfully boring to look at. Who will buy it? Now you add a few bells and whistles. They don't do anything useful, but they make the product more interesting. Nobody seems to know what distinguishes a bell from a whistle.

BIGNUM *(big'num) noun.*
1. A multiple-precision computer representation for very large integers.
2. More generally, any very large number. "Have you ever looked at the United States Budget? There's bignums for you!"
3. When playing backgammon, large numbers on the dice, especially a roll of double fives or double sixes.

See EL CAMINO BIGNUM.

Most computer languages provide a kind of data called "integer," but such computer integers are usually very limited in size; usually they must be smaller than 2^{15} (32768) or 2^{31} (2147483648). If you want to work with numbers larger than that, you have to use floating-point numbers, which are usually only accurate to six or seven decimal places.

Computer languages that provide bignums can perform exact calculations on very large numbers such as 2^{1000} or 1000! (the factorial of 1000, which is 1000 times 999 times 998 times . . . times 2 times 1) exactly. For example, this value for 1000! was computed by the MACLISP system using bignums:

402387260077093773543702433923003985719374864210714632543799910429938512398629020592044208486969404800479988610197196058631666872994808558901323829669944590997424504087073759918823627272188732519779505950995276120874975462497043601418278094646496291056393887437886487337119181045825783647849977012476632889835955735432513185323958463075557409114262417474349347553428646576611667797396668820291207379143853719588249808126867838374559731746136085379534

52422158659320192809087829730843139284440328123155
86110369768013573042161687476096758713483120254785
89320767169132448426236131412508780208000261683151
02734182797770478463586817016436502415369139828126
48102130927612448963599287051149649754199093422215
66832572080821333186116811553615836546984046708975
60290095053761647584772842188967964624494516076535
34081989013854424879849599533191017233555566021394
50399736280750137837615307127761926849034352625200
01588853514733161170210396817592151090778801939317
81141945452572238655414610628921879602238389714760
88506276862967146674697562911234082439208160153780
88989396451826324367161676217916890977991190375403
12746222899880051954444142820121873617459926429565
81746628302955570299024324153181617210465832036786
90611726015878352075151628422554026517048330422614
39742869330616908979684825901254583271682264580665
26769958652682272807075781391858178889652208164348
34482599326604336766017699961283186078838615027946
59551311565520360939881806121385586003014356945272
24206344631797460594682573103790084024432438465657
24501440282188525247093519062092902313649327349756
55139587205596542287497740114133469627154228458623
77387538230483865688976419273838149001407673104466
64025989949022222176590433990188601856652648506179
97023561938970178600408118897299183110211712298459
01641921068884387121855646124960798722908519296819
37238864261483965738229112312502418664935314397013
74285319266498753372189406942814341185201580141233
44828015051399694290153483077644569099073152433278
28826986460278986432113908350621709500259738986355
42771967428222487575867657523442202075736305694988
25087968928162753848863396909959826280956121450994
87170124451646126037902930912088908694202851064018
21543994571568059418727489980942547421735824010636
77404595741785160829230135358081840096996372524230
56085590370062427124341690900415369010593398383577
79394109700277534720000000000000000000000000000000

00000000000000000000000000000000000000000000000000
00000000000000000000000000000000000000000000000000
00000000000000000000000000000000000000000000000000
00000000000000000000000000000000000000000000000000
000000000000000000

The MACLISP language was not the first computer system to calculate very large integers, but it was MACLISP that provided the name "bignum."

BIT *noun.*
1. The unit of information: the amount of information obtained by asking a yes-or-no question.
2. A computational quantity that can take on one of two values, such as true and false, or 0 and 1.
3. A mental flag: a reminder that something should be done eventually. Example: "I have a bit set for you." (I haven't seen you for a while, and I'm supposed to tell or ask you something.)

A bit is said to be "set" if its value is true or 1, and "reset" or "clear" if its value is false or 0. One speaks of setting and clearing bits. To TOGGLE a bit is to change it, either from 0 to 1 or from 1 to 0.

BITS. Information. Examples: "I need some bits about file formats." ("I need to know about file formats.")

THE SOURCE OF ALL GOOD BITS. *noun.* A person from whom (or a place from which) information may be obtained. If you need to know about a program, a WIZARD might be the source of all good bits. The title is often applied to a particularly competent secretary.

BITBLT *(bit'blit)*
1. *verb.* To copy a large array of bits from one part of a computer's memory to another part, particularly when the memory is being used to determine what is shown on a display screen.
2. More generally, to perform some operation (such as TOGGLING) on a large array of bits while moving them.
3. *noun.* The operation of bitblting.

See BLT.

BIT BUCKET *noun.*
1. The mythical receptacle used to catch bits when they fall off the end of a register during a shift instruction.
2. More generally, the place where information goes when it is lost or destroyed. Example: "Oh, no! All my files just went into the bit bucket!"
3. The physical device used to implement output to the NULL DEVICE.
   This term is used purely in jest. It's based on the fanciful notion that bits are objects that are not destroyed, only misplaced.

BIT DECAY *noun.*
A fanciful theory to explain SOFTWARE ROT, the phenomenon that unused programs or features will eventually stop working even if "nothing has changed." The theory explains that bits decay as if they were radioactive. As time passes, the contents of a file or the code in a program will become increasingly garbled.

There actually are physical processes that produce these effects. Alpha particles, such as those found in cosmic rays, can change the contents of a computer memory unpredictably. Fortunately, the probability of this can be kept fairly low. In any case, when you can't figure out why something stopped working, it is often convenient to blame it on bit decay.

BLETCH *(bletch) interjection.*
Term of disgust.
   BLETCHEROUS *adjective.*   Disgusting in design or function, aesthetically unappealing. (This word is seldom used of people.) Example: "This keyboard is bletcherous!" (Perhaps the keys don't work very well or are poorly arranged.) *Slightly comic.*

"Bletcherous" applies to the aesthetics of the thing so described; similarly for CRETINOUS. By contrast, something that is LOSING or BAGBITING may be failing to meet objective criteria. See BOGUS and RANDOM, which have richer and wider shades of meaning than any of the others.

BLT *(blit, belt) verb.*

To copy or transfer a large contiguous package of information from one place to another. "The storage allocator picks through the table and copies the good parts up into high memory, and at the end blt's it all back down again."

THE BIG BLT *noun.* A massive memory-shuffling operation frequently performed by some time-sharing systems on the PDP-10 computer.

This comes from the name of a PDP-10 instruction that copies a block of memory from one place to another; the name "BLT" stands for "Block Transfer." Nowadays, BLT almost always means "Branch if Less Than zero," so the slang meanings above are rather like antiques or dinosaurs.

BOGUS *(boh'guss) adjective.*
1. Nonfunctional. Example: "Your fix for that BUG was bogus."
2. Useless. Example: "ATSIGN is a bogus program."
3. False. Example: "Your arguments are bogus."
4. Incorrect. Example: "That algorithm is bogus."
5. Unbelievable. Example: "You claim to have solved the halting problem for Turing Machines? That's totally bogus."
6. Silly. Example: "Stop writing those bogus SAGAS."
Astrology is bogus. So is a bolt that is obviously about to break. So is someone who makes blatantly false claims of having solved a scientific problem.

BOGOSITY *(boh-gahss':t-ee) noun.* The quality of being bogus; also, an instance or example thereof.

BOGON *(boh'gahn) noun.*
1. A person who is bogus or who says bogus things.
2. More rarely, a mythical subatomic particle that bears the unit charge of bogosity. (A convention in particle physics is to name new subatomic particles by using the Greek suffix *-on*, because Greek words were originally used to name such particles. For example, hadrons are very massive particles that were named from the Greek word *hadros,* meaning "heavy." More recently, however, physicists have taken to attaching this suffix to words from other languages. For example, the particles that help to hold quarks together are

called "gluons," from the English word *glue*. Hackers have used this convention in fun, on an *ad hoc* basis; but two of them, "bogon" and COMPUTRON, are used fairly regularly.)

BOGOMETER *(boh-gahm':t-:r) noun.* A mythical instrument used to measure bogosity, much as a thermometer measures temperature. Example: In a seminar, when a speaker makes an outrageous claim, a listener might raise his hand and say, "My bogometer just triggered."

Someone who is a bogon in the first sense probably radiates a lot of bogons in the second sense. This provides a (pseudo) scientific explanation for how a bogometer works: it's like a Geiger counter that detects bogons.

The agreed-upon unit of bogosity is the microLenat (uL) or one-millionth of a Lenat, in honor of computer scientist Doug Lenat. The consensus is that this is the largest unit practical for everyday use.

BOGOTIFY *(boh-gaht':f-ie) verb.* To make or become bogus. A program that has been changed so many times as to become completely disorganized has become bogotified. If you tighten a nut too hard and strip the threads on the bolt, the bolt has become bogotified and you'd better not use it any more.

BOGUE OUT *(bohg owt) verb.* To become bogus, suddenly and unexpectedly. Example: "His talk was relatively sane, but then someone asked him a tricky question; he bogued out and did nothing but FLAME after that."

AUTOBOGOTIPHOBIA *(aw'to-boh-gaht':-foh'bee-uh) noun.* The fear of becoming bogotified.

"Bogus" has many, but not all, of the meanings of RANDOM. "Random" tends to connote pointlessness or a lack of direction, while "bogus" tends to connote deception or misdirection. Both, however, may connote confusion.

"Bogus" was originally used in the hacker sense at Princeton in the late 1960s; not just in the computer science department but all over campus. It came to Yale and (we assume) elsewhere through the efforts of migratory Princeton alumni,

Michael Shamos in particular, now a faculty member at CMU. The hacker usage of this word has since spread to other places.

BOUNCE *verb.*
To play volleyball.
This term is, or was, used primarily at Stanford. At one time there was a volleyball court next to the computer laboratory. From 5:00 P.M. to 7:00 P.M. was the scheduled maintenance time for the computer, so every afternoon at 5:00 the computer would become unavailable. And over the intercom a voice would cry, "Bounce, bounce!" meaning "Everyone come out and play volleyball!"

BRAIN-DAMAGED *adjective.*
Obviously wrong; extremely poorly designed; CRETINOUS; DEMENTED.
There is a connotation that the person responsible must have suffered brain damage, because he should have known better. Calling something brain-damaged is really extreme. The word implies that the thing is completely unusable, and that its failure to work is due to poor design, not accident.

BREAK *verb.*
1. To become BROKEN (in any sense).
2. To cause to be broken (in any sense). "Your latest patch to the editor broke the paragraph commands."
3. Of a program, to halt or pause temporarily so that it may be examined for debugging purposes. The place where the program stops is called a "breakpoint." See CONTROL-B.

BROKEN *adjective.*
1. Of programs, not working properly. "The FORTRAN compiler is broken."
2. Behaving strangely—especially (of people), exhibiting extreme depression.

BROKET *(broh'k:t, broh'ket) noun.*
Either of the characters " < " and " > ". The first is called a "left broket," and the second a "right broket."

This word originated as a contraction of the phrase "broken bracket," that is, a bracket that is bent in the middle.

BUCKY BITS *noun.*

Bits corresponding to "control" and "meta" keys on a keyboard.

See DOUBLE BUCKY and QUADRUPLE BUCKY.

This phrase requires a long explanation. Most computer keyboards are arranged more or less like a typewriter keyboard, but have extra keys. One of them, usually marked "control" or "CTRL," is like a shift key, but instead of changing letters from lower case to upper case, it changes them into so-called control characters. The character sent when you hold down the control key and type *F* is called simply "control-F." Such characters are usually used as commands to the computer, especially to a text editor. In one well-known text editor, EMACS (which was written at MIT), control-F moves forward one character, control-N moves to the next line, control-P moves to the previous line, control-D deletes a character, and so on.

Control characters are so useful that sometimes special keyboards are built that have even more shift keys. One of the first of these was used at Stanford. It had the usual shift and control keys, and a third key called "meta," as well as lots of unusual characters such as Greek letters. So, one can type such characters as control-F, meta-N, and control-meta-B.

Now, when you type a character on a Stanford keyboard, the following information is sent to the computer: a code indicating the basic character, plus one BIT for each shifting key to indicate whether that shifting key was pressed along with the basic character key. Programs usually treat the regular shift key as part of the basic character, indicating whether you want lower case or upper case (or whether you want "3" or "#", and so on). The other bits (control and meta) are called the bucky bits.

Why "bucky"? Rumor has it that the idea for extra bits for characters came from computer scientist Niklaus Wirth (who invented the computer languages PASCAL and MODULA-2) when he was at Stanford, and that his nickname was "Bucky."

Inspired by the Stanford keyboard, the MIT SPACE CADET

KEYBOARD has seven shifting keys: four "bucky bit" keys—"control," "meta," "hyper," and "super"—and three like the regular shift key, called "shift," "top," and "front." Many keys have three symbols on them: a letter and a symbol on the top, and a Greek letter on the front. For example, the *L* key has an "L" and a two-way arrow on the top, and the Greek letter lambda on the front. If you press this key with the right hand while playing an appropriate "chord" with the left hand on the shift keys, you can get the following results:

L	lower-case "l"
shift-L	upper-case "L"
front-L	Greek lower-case lambda "λ"
front-shift-L	Greek upper-case lambda "Λ"
top-L (front and shift are ignored)	two-way arrow

And of course each of these may also be typed with any combination of the control, meta, hyper, and super keys. On this keyboard you can type over 8000 different characters! This allows the user to type very complicated mathematical text, and also to have thousands of single-character commands at his disposal. Many hackers are actually willing to memorize the command meanings of that many characters if it will reduce typing time. Other hackers, however, think having that many bucky bits is overkill, and object that such a keyboard can require three or four hands to operate.

BUG *noun.*

A mistake or problem (possibly simple, possibly very deep); an unwanted and unintended property, characteristic, or behavior. Examples: "There's a bug in the editor. It writes things out backward." "The system CRASHED because of a hardware bug." (That is, the computer suddenly stopped because of an equipment failure.) "Fred is a WINNER, but he has a few bugs." (Fred is a good guy, but he has a few personality problems.)

Antonym: FEATURE.

This is usually thought of as applying to a program, but can be applied to computers, people, and other things.

Some say this term came from telephone company usage: "Bugs in a telephone cable" were blamed for noisy lines. However, computer scientist Grace Hopper has repeatedly been heard to claim that the use of the term in computer science comes from a story concerning actual bugs found wedged in an early malfunctioning computer. In any case, in hacker's slang the word almost never refers to insects. Here is a plausible conversation that never actually happened:

"This ant farm has a bug."
"What do you mean? There aren't even any ants in it."
"That's the bug."

BUM

1. *verb.* To improve something by removing or rearranging its parts—such as wires in a computer or instructions from a program—while preserving its function. More generally, to make highly efficient, either in time or space. The connotation is that this is done at the expense of clarity. Examples: "I managed to bum three more instructions out of that code." "I bummed the program not to write the file if it would be empty." "I bummed the inner loop of the program down to seven microseconds."

2. *noun.* A small change to an algorithm, program, or object to make it more efficient. "This hardware bum makes the jump instruction faster."

BUZZ *verb.*

Of a program, to run with no indication of progress and perhaps without guarantee of ever finishing. The state of a buzzing program resembles CATATONIA, but you never get out of catatonia, while a buzzing loop may eventually end of its own accord. Example: "The program buzzes for about ten seconds trying to sort all the names into order."

CANONICAL *(ki-nahn'i-kil) adjective.*

Usual; standard; ordinary. Example: "What is the canonical way to rejustify a paragraph in EMACS?"

This word has a somewhat more technical meaning in mathematics. For example, one sometimes speaks of a formula as being in canonical form. Two formulas such as $9+3x^2+x$ and $3x^2+x+9$ are said to be equivalent because they mean the same thing, but the second one is in canonical form because it is written in the usual way, with the highest power of x first. Usually there are fixed rules you can use to decide whether something is in canonical form. The slang meaning is a relaxation of the technical meaning.

A true story: One Bob Sjoberg, new at MIT, expressed some annoyance at the use of hacker's slang. Over his loud objections, we made a point of using the slang as much as possible in his presence, and eventually it began to sink in. Finally, in one conversation he used the word "canonical" in slanglike fashion without thinking.

Steele: Aha! We've finally got him talking jargon [slang] too!
Stallman: (who wasn't quite paying attention) What did he say?
Steele: Bob just used "canonical" in the canonical way.

CATATONIA *(kat':-toh'nee-uh) noun.*
A condition of suspended animation in which something is so WEDGED that it makes no response. For example, if you are typing on your terminal and suddenly the computer doesn't even make the letters appear on the screen as you type—let alone do what you're asking it to do—then the computer is suffering from catatonia (probably because it has CRASHED).
  CATATONIC *(kat':-tahn'ik) adjective.*   In a state of catatonia. Synonym: WEDGED.

CDR *(ku'd:r) verb.*
To remove the first item from a list of things.
  CDR DOWN *verb.*   To go down a list of things one by one. Example: "Shall we cdr down the agenda?" *Silly.*
  This term is derived from a function of the LISP language that removes an item from a list.

CHARACTERS *noun.*
Those things that you type on a keyboard or that appear on your terminal. (Sometimes you can type characters on your

keyboard that cannot be printed on the screen, and vice versa. For example, on most keyboards you can type "control characters" that can't be written down like the characters "A" and "%" can; they are mostly used as special commands. Conversely, some terminals can display almost any picture a program can draw. A program can then draw Greek letters or any other funny symbol, even if they aren't on the keyboard.)

Computers tend to seem very unforgiving: a program can fail to work if you get even one character in it wrong. (Folklore has it that a NASA mission to Venus failed because, in one place in one program, there was a period where there should have been a comma.) Hackers therefore need to be very precise when talking about characters, and have developed a considerable amount of verbal shorthand for talking about characters:

!	EXCL, exclam, BANG, SHRIEK, WOW.
#	Hash mark, MESH, SPLAT, CRUNCH, pig-pen.
$	Dollar.
&	Ampersand. (This name is already so silly that no slang term is needed!)
'	Single quote, forward quote.
(and)	Parens (separately called just OPEN and CLOSE).
*	Star, SPLAT. (In other computer communities, the name "gear" is used, because it looks like a little cogwheel.)
.	Period, dot, point. (Which of these is used depends on culture and context. The word "point" is used more at MIT than "dot" is. CMU uses "dot" almost exclusively.)
/	Slash, forward slash.
;	SEMI.
<	Less than, left ANGLE BRACKET, open angle bracket, left BROKET.
=	Equals.
>	Greater than, right ANGLE BRACKET, close angle bracket, right BROKET.
?	QUES, query.

@   At-sign, at.
\   Backslash.
^   Caret. (The name "uparrow" is also used; this dates
            from the days of old ASCII, when the code now
            assigned to circumflex was used for an upward-
            pointing arrow.)
_   Backarrow. (This dates from the days of old ASCII,
            when the code now assigned to underscore used to
            be used for a leftward-pointing arrow.)
`   Backquote.
{ and }   Curly braces, curly brackets, SQUIGGLE BRACKETS.
| Vertical bar.
~   TWIDDLE, SQUIGGLE, SQIGGLE.

The INTERCAL programming language, consistent with its
general policy of never doing anything the way some other
programming language does it, has odd names especially invented for many characters. Most of these names are generally
not used except in the context of INTERCAL:

.   Spot.
:   Two-spot.
,   Tail.
Mesh.
=   Half-mesh.
'   Spark.
`   Backspark.
"   Rabbit ears.
!   WOW.
?   What.
| Spike.
—   Worm.
<   Angle. (The two-character arrow " < — " is called
            "angleworm.")
>   Right angle.
(Wax.
)   Wane.
[U turn.

]	U turn back.
{	Embrace.
}	Bracelet.
*	SPLAT.
&	Ampersand. (INTERCAL couldn't make this any sillier, either.)
—	Flatworm.
+	Intersection.
/	Slat.
\	Backslat.
^	Shark (or simply shark fin).
@	Whirlpool.
%	Double-oh-seven.

CHINE NUAL *(sheen'yu-:l) noun.*

The reference manual for the Lisp Machine, a computer designed at MIT especially for running the LISP language. It is called this because the title, LISP MACHINE MANUAL, appears in big block letters—wrapped around the cover in such a way that you have to open the cover out flat to see the whole thing. If you look at just the front cover, you see only part of the title, and it reads "LISP CHINE NUAL."

CHOMP *(chahmp) verb.*

To LOSE; to chew on something of which more was bitten off than one can.

Synonyms: LOSE, BITE THE BAG (see BAGBITER).

A hand gesture commonly accompanies the use of the word "chomp." The four fingers are held together as if in a mitten or hand puppet, and the fingers and thumb are opened and closed rapidly to illustrate a biting action. The hand may be pointed at the object of complaint, and for real emphasis you can use both hands at once. For example, to do this to a person is equivalent to saying, "You chomper!" If you point the gesture at yourself, it is a humble but humorous admission of some failure. I would do this if someone told me that a program I had written had failed in some surprising way and I felt stupid for not having anticipated it.

CHOMPER *(chahmp':r) noun.* Someone or something that is chomping; a loser.

Synonyms: LOSER, BAGBITER.

CLOSE *(klohz)*

1. *adjective.* Of a delimiting CHARACTER, used at the right-hand end of a grouping. Used in such terms as "close parenthesis" and "close bracket."
2. *noun.* Abbreviation for "close (or right) parenthesis," used when necessary to eliminate oral ambiguity. See OPEN and CHARACTERS.
3. *verb.* To terminate one's interaction with a file of information. See OPEN.

COKEBOTTLE *(kohk'baht-:l) noun.*

Any very unusual character, particularly one that isn't on your keyboard so you can't type it. A program written at Stanford, for example, is likely to have a lot of "control-meta-cokebottle" commands, that is, commands that you can only type on a Stanford keyboard—because you need the "control" and "meta" keys (see BUCKY BITS)—and also unusual characters such as the downward-pointing arrow. The last is a "cokebottle" unless you happen to have a Stanford keyboard. (This usage probably arose because of the unusual and distinctive shape of Coca-Cola bottles. No keyboard I know of actually has a cokebottle character on it, so any character you can't type might as well be a Coke bottle for all the good it does you.)

COM MODE, COMM MODE *(kahm' mohd) noun.*

A situation in which two or more terminals are linked together by the computer so that whatever is typed on any of them appears on all of them. Ideally this is accomplished in such a way that what you type appears on the other terminals but is not otherwise interpreted by the computer (so what you type doesn't foul up your programs). The word *com* is short for *communicate.*

Com mode is used for conversation: you can talk to other hackers without leaving your terminal. It combines the immediacy of talking with all the precision (and verbosity) that

written language entails. It is difficult to communicate inflec-
tions, though conventions have arisen for some of these. For
example, to emphasize a word (as if printed in italics), one may
type an asterisk before and after the word. Typing in all-capital
letters is equivalent to raising one's voice.

Neophytes, when in com mode, seem to think they must
produce letter-perfect prose because they are typing rather
than speaking. This is not the best approach. It can be very
frustrating to wait while your partner pauses to think of a word,
or repeatedly makes the same spelling error and backs up to
fix it. It is usually best just to leave typographical errors behind
and plunge forward, unless severe confusion may result. In that
case, it is often fastest just to type xxx and start over from
before the mistake.

There is a special set of slang terms used only in com mode,
which are not used vocally. These are used to save typing or
to communicate inflection.

BCNU	Be seeing you (that is, good-bye).
BTW	By the way . . .
BYE?	Are you ready to unlink? (This is the standard way to end a com mode conversation: the other person types BYE to confirm, or else continues the conversation.)
CUL	See you later.
FOO?	A greeting, also meaning R U THERE? Often used in the case of unexpected links, meaning also "Sorry if I butted in" (linker) or "What's up?" (linkee).
FYI	For your information . . .
GA	Go ahead (used when two people have tried to type simultaneously; this cedes the right to type to the other).
HELLOP	A greeting, also meaning R U THERE? (This is an instance of the -P convention.)
NIL	No. (See the main entry for NIL.)
OBTW	Oh, by the way . . .
R U THERE?	Are you there?

SEC	Wait a second (sometimes written SEC . . .). For example, if you are interrupted by a telephone call, or need to think about something before replying, you might type this. You might also type an additional dot every few seconds to indicate that you are still there but busy. Also, if you need to use a program for a moment (possibly because someone asked you a question), you might type SEC . . . , unlink your terminal, use your program, and then link back into the com mode.
T	Yes. (See the main entry for T.)
TNX	Thanks.
TNX 1.0E6	Thanks a million. (This "1.0E6" is a standard way to write one million in many computer languages.) *Silly*.
[double crlf]	When the typing party has finished, he types two CRLF's (that is, presses the RETURN key twice) to signal that he is done. This leaves a blank line between individual "speeches" in the conversation, making it easier to reread the preceding text, and indicates that the other person may type.
[name]:	When three or more terminals are linked, each speech is preceded by the typist's login name ("computer id") and a colon (or a hyphen) to indicate who is typing. You need to do this because you can't tell who is who by tone of voice! The login name often is shortened to a unique prefix (possibly a single letter) during a very long conversation.
/\/\/\	The equivalent of a giggle.

Synonym: TALK MODE. (The term "com mode" is used more at MIT, and "talk mode" at Stanford.)

COMPUTRON *(kahm'pyoo-trahn').* **COMPUTON** *(kahm'pyoo-tahn')* *noun.*

A mythical subatomic particle that bears the unit quantity of computation or information, in much the same way that an electron bears one unit of electric charge. If the computer is too slow, it's because you're short of computrons. See BOGON and CYCLE.

An elaborate pseudo-scientific theory of computrons has been worked out as a jest by MIT hacker Stavros Macrakis. (He called the particles "mensons," but that name is no longer used.) It is a well-known fact of physics that as you heat something, the molecules get jiggled around and their positions become more random. The hotter it gets, the less predictable are the positions of the molecules. Eventually the molecules just spill all over each other, and the thing melts. Now, he argues, it obviously melts because each molecule has lost the information about where it is supposed to be: in other words, it has lost computrons. This explains why computers get so hot and require air conditioning: they use up computrons. Conversely, you should be able to refrigerate something simply by placing it in the path of a computron beam.

CMU hacker Joe Newcomer has also observed that this theory explains why a computer works when it's tested in the factory but not when you've put it in the computer room with all the other computers. They're tested singly at the factory, and so there are plenty of computrons available there, but in the computer room all the computers compete for the computrons in a limited space and some of them come up short.

CONNECTOR CONSPIRACY *noun.*

The (perhaps only mythical) tendency of manufacturers (or, by extension, programmers or purveyors of anything) to come up with new products that don't fit together with the old stuff, thereby making you buy either all new stuff or expensive interface devices.

This term probably came into prominence with the appearance of the KL 10 model of PDP-10, none of whose connectors seemed to match anything else.

CONS *(kahnz) verb.*
To add a new element to a list, usually to the top rather than at the bottom.

CONS UP *verb.* To synthesize from smaller pieces; more generally, to create or invent. Examples: "I'm trying to cons up a list of volleyball players." "Let's cons up an example."

This term comes from the LISP programming language, which has a function called CONS that adds a data item to the front of a list.

CONTROL
The name of one of the several BUCKY BITS. Used as a prefix to another character, it indicates that the "control" key on your keyboard should be pressed as the other character is typed.

CONTROL-B *(k:n-trohl' bee') interjection.*
May I interrupt? or, Beginning of digression. Synonym: PUSH. Antonym: CONTROL-P.

CONTROL-G *(k: n-trohl' jee') interjection.*
Stop! Cease! Change the subject! Stop that FLAMING!

CONTROL-P *(k: n-trohl' pee') interjection.*
End of interruption or digression. If two hackers are sitting in an office talking, a third one might stick his head in the door and ask "Control-B?" This is a polite, albeit silly, way of asking "May I interrupt?" When the side conversation is done, the third hacker might say, "Thanks a lot. Control-P!"

Control characters are used in various ways to control the actions of computer programs. Different computer systems have different conventions about how control characters are used, and hackers will use the local computer convention when speaking. The definitions given above correspond to their meanings as used in the MACLISP language and in DDT at MIT. At other places "Control-C" replaces "Control-G," for example.

CRASH
1. *noun.* A sudden, usually drastic failure. Most often said of the SYSTEM, sometimes of magnetic disk drives. Example: "Three LUSERS lost their files in last night's disk crash." The

term "system crash" usually, though not always, implies that the operating system or other software was at fault. Disk crashes come in two varieties: either the disks are physically unharmed but some information stored on them is lost, or else the disks are physically damaged—in which case the entire information content of the disk is usually lost. The second kind usually occurs when the magnetic read/write heads hit the surfaces of the disks and scrape off the oxide. This kind of disk crash is called a "head crash."

2. *verb.* To fail suddenly. Example: "Has the system just crashed?"

3. *verb.* To cause to fail. Example: "There is a BUG in the tape controller; if you try to use the tape drive, you will crash the system."

4. *verb.* Of people, to go to sleep—particularly after a long period of work. See GRONK OUT.

CREEPING FEATURISM *(kreep'eeng feetch':r-iz':m) noun.*
The tendency for anything complicated to become even more complicated because people keep saying, "Gee, it would be even better if it had this feature too." (See FEATURE.) The result is usually a patchwork, because it grew one *ad hoc* step at a time, rather than being planned. Planning is a lot of work, but it's easy to add just one extra little feature to help someone. . . . And then another . . . and another. . . . Usually this term is used to describe computer programs, but it could also be applied to the federal government, the IRS 1040 form, and new cars.

CRETIN *(kreet-:n) noun*
A congenital LOSER; an obnoxious person; someone who can't do anything right.

  CRETINOUS *(kree'tin-uhss, kreet':n-uhss) adjective.* Wrong; nonfunctional; very poorly designed (also used pejoratively of people).

  Synonyms: BLETCHEROUS, BAGBITING, LOSING, BRAIN-DAMAGED.

CRLF *(k:r'lif, crul':f)*
1. *noun.* A carriage return (CR) followed by a line feed (LF).

More loosely, whatever it takes to get you from the end of one line of text to the beginning of the next line.

2. *verb.* To output a crlf; to end a line of text or to begin a new line of text.

Synonym: TERPRI.

CROCK *noun.*

1. Something, especially a program, that works but does so in an unbelievably ugly or awkward manner; more specifically, something that works acceptably but which is quite prone to failure if disturbed in the least.
2. A tightly woven, almost completely unmodifiable structure; something very complicated that ought to be simple.

Computer programs seldom stay the same forever. They tend to evolve, and are constantly changed as BUGS are fixed or new FEATURES added. Crocks make this difficult because, although they work, they are very difficult to make small changes to.

Synonym: KLUDGE.

CROCKISH, CROCKY *adjective.* Having the characteristics of a crock. See BLETCHEROUS.

CROCKITUDE *(krahk':-tood) noun.* Crockness, crockhood.

CRUFT *(kruhft)*

1. *noun.* An unpleasant substance. The dust that gathers under your bed is cruft.
2. *noun.* The results of shoddy construction.

CRUFT TOGETHER *verb.* To make something quickly and haphazardly to get it working quickly, without regard to craftsmanship. Example: "There isn't any program now to reverse all the lines of a file, but I can probably cruft one together in about ten minutes."

The origin of this word is unknown.

CRUFTY *(kruhft'ee)*

1. *adjective.* Unpleasant, especially to the touch; yucky, like spilled coffee smeared with peanut butter and catsup.
2. *adjective.* Poorly built, possibly overly complex. "This is standard old crufty DEC software."

3. *adjective.* Generally unpleasant.

4. *noun* (also spelled "cruftie"). A small crufty object, or (in a program) a small data structure, especially one that doesn't fit well into the scheme of things. Every desk seems to have one drawer that accumulates crufties. Example: "A LISP property list is a good place to store crufties." (In the LISP language, odd data structures can be stored in a catchall data structure called a property list.)

CRUFTSMANSHIP *noun.*   The antithesis of craftsmanship.

CRUNCH

1. *verb.* To process, usually in a time-consuming or complicated way. The connotation is of an essentially trivial operation that is nonetheless painful to perform, possibly because the trivial operation must be performed millions of times. When the trivial operation involves numerical computation, this is called "number crunching." Example: "FORTRAN programs mostly do number crunching."

2. *verb.* To reduce the size of a file by a complicated scheme that produces bit configurations completely unrelated to the original data, such as by the mathematical technique called "Huffman codes." (The file ends up looking like a paper document would if somebody crunched the paper into a wad.) Since such a compression operation usually requires a great deal of computation (it is much more sophisticated than such simpler methods as counting consecutive repeated characters), the term is doubly appropriate. Sometimes the term "file crunching" is used to distinguish it from "number crunching."

3. *noun.* A crisis, especially a scarcity of some resource. If you don't have much time to get something done, you're in a time crunch. See CYCLE CRUNCH.

4. *noun.* The character " # ". See CHARACTERS.

CTY *(sit′ee) noun.*

The terminal physically associated with a computer's operating console. The term is a contraction of "Console TTY," that is, "Console TeleTYpe."

CUSPY *(cuhsp'ee) adjective.*
Clean; well-written; functionally excellent. A program that performs well and interfaces well to users is cuspy.
Antonyms: RUDE, CRUFTY, BLETCHEROUS.
This term originated at WPI. It comes from the acronym CUSP, used by DEC to mean a "Commonly Used System Program," that is, a utility program used by many people. Ideally, such programs, whatever the source, are built to high standards of excellence. The extent to which a hacker uses this word obviously depends largely on how highly he regards DEC-supplied software.

CYCLE *noun.*
The "basic unit of computation." What every hacker wants more of.
You might think that single machine instructions would be the measure of computation, and indeed computers are often compared by assessing how many instructions they can process per second—even though some instructions take longer than others. Nearly all computers have an internal clock, though, and you can describe an instruction as taking so many "clock cycles." Typically the computer can access its memory once on every clock cycle, and so one speaks also of "memory cycles." These are technical meanings of "cycle."
The slang meaning comes from the observation that there are only so many cycles per second; and when you are sharing a computer, the cycles get divided up among the users. The more cycles the computer spends working on your program rather than someone else's, the faster your program will run. That's why every hacker wants more cycles: so he can spend less time waiting for the computer to respond.
CYCLE CRUNCH *noun.* The situation where the number of people simultaneously trying to use the computer has reached the point where no one can get enough cycles because they are spread too thin. Usually the only solution is to buy another computer.
CYCLE DROUGHT *noun.* A scarcity of cycles. It may be due to a cycle crunch, but could also occur because part of the

computer is temporarily not working, leaving fewer cycles to go around. Example: "The high MOBY is DOWN, so we're running with only half the usual amount of memory. There will be a cycle drought until it's fixed."

DAEMON *(day'm:n, dee'm:n) noun.*

A program that is not invoked explicitly, but that lies dormant waiting for one or more conditions to occur. The idea is that the perpetrator of the condition need not be aware that a daemon is lurking (though often a program will commit an action only because it knows that it will implicitly invoke a daemon). For example, many operating systems have a printing daemon. When you want to print a file on some printing device, instead of explicitly running a program that does the printing, you just copy your file to a particular directory (file area). The printer daemon is just a program that is always running; it checks the special directory periodically, and whenever it finds a file there it prints it and then deletes it. The advantage is that programs that want (in this example) files printed need not compete for access to the printing device itself, and need not wait until the printing process is completed. In particular, a user doesn't have to sit there waiting with his terminal tied up while the printing program does its work. He can do something else useful while the daemon does its job.

Daemon and DEMON are often used interchangeably, but seem to have discrete connotations. "Daemon" was introduced to computing by people working on CTSS, the Compatible Time-Sharing System, which was the first time-sharing system, developed at MIT. They pronounced it "dee'm:n," and used it to refer to what is now called a DRAGON or PHANTOM. The meaning and pronunciation have drifted, and we think the definitions given here reflect current usage.

DAY MODE *noun.*

The state a person is in when he is working during the day and sleeping at night.

See PHASE and NIGHT MODE.

DDT *(dee'dee'tee')* *noun.*

A program that helps you to debug other programs by showing individual machine instructions in a readable symbolic form and letting the user change them. At MIT, DDT is also used as the "top-level command language" to run other programs.

The *DEC PDP-10 Reference Handbook* (1969) contained this footnote on the first page of the documentation for DDT:

Historical footnote: DDT was developed at MIT for the PDP-1 computer in 1961. At that time DDT stood for "DEC Debugging Tape." Since then, the idea of an on-line debugging program has propagated throughout the computer industry. DDT programs are now available for all DEC computers. Since media other than tape are now frequently used, the more descriptive name "Dynamic Debugging Technique" has been adopted, retaining the DDT acronym. Confusion between DDT-10 and another well-known pesticide, dichloro-diphenyl-trichloroethane ($C_{14}H_9Cl_5$) should be minimal, since each attacks a different, and apparently mutually exclusive, class of bugs.

Sad to say, this quotation was removed from later editions of the handbook as DEC became much more "businesslike."

DEADLOCK *noun.*

A situation wherein two or more processes (or persons) are unable to proceed because each is waiting for another to do something.

Here is a typical example: Two programs running on the same computer both want the exclusive use of two things, say a line printer and a disk. The first one grabs the line printer and then tries to grab the disk, but fails because the second one successfully grabbed the disk and is now waiting to get the line printer.

Deadlock also occurs when two people meet in a narrow corridor and each tries to be polite by moving aside to let the other pass—but they end up swaying from side to side without making any progress because they always move the same way at the same time.

Synonym: DEADLY EMBRACE.

DEADLY EMBRACE *noun.*

DEADLOCK. This term is usually used only when exactly two processes are involved, while "deadlock" can involve any number. Also, "deadly embrace" seems to be the more popular term in Europe, while "deadlock" is more frequently used in the United States.

DELTA *noun.*

1. A change, especially a small or incremental change. Example: "I just doubled the speed of my program!" "What was the delta on program size?" "About thirty percent." (He doubled the speed of his program, but increased its size by thirty percent.)

2. A small quantity, but not so small as EPSILON.

DEMENTED *adjective.*

Useless; totally nonfunctional; BRAIN-DAMAGED.

This is yet another term of disgust used to describe a program. The connotation in this case is that the program works as designed, but the design is bad; perhaps also that the program explicitly exhibits strange behavior. For example, a program that generates large numbers of meaningless error messages, implying that it is on the point of imminent collapse, would be described as demented.

DEMON *(dee'm:n) noun.*

A portion of a program which is not invoked explicitly, but which lies dormant waiting for some condition(s) to occur. See DAEMON.

Demons are usually processes that are pieces of a single program, while daemons are usually entire programs running in the context of a large system, such as an operating system. This distinction is admittedly not hard and fast. Demons are particularly common in artificial intelligence programs. For example, a knowledge manipulation program might implement inference rules as demons. Whenever a new piece of knowledge was added, various demons would activate (which demons depends on the particular piece of data) and would create additional pieces of knowledge by applying their respective inference rules to the original piece. These new pieces could in turn activate more demons as the inferences filtered down through chains of logic. Meanwhile the main program could continue with whatever its primary task was.

DIDDLE *(did':l)*

1. *verb.* To work with in a not particularly serious manner; to make a very simple change (as to a program). Examples: "Let's diddle this piece of code and see if the problem goes away." (That is, let's try the obvious quick fix.) "I diddled the text editor to ring the bell before it deletes all your files."
2. *noun.* The action or result of diddling.

Synonyms: TWEAK, TWIDDLE.

DIKE *(diek) verb.*

To remove or disable a portion of something, as a wire from a computer or a subroutine from a program.

A standard slogan: "When in doubt, dike it out." (The implication is that the program [or whatever] is so bad that taking something out can only make things better!)

The word "dikes" is widely used among mechanics and engineers to mean "diagonal cutters," a heavy-duty metal cutting device. To "dike something out" means to use such cutters to remove something. Among hackers, this term has been metaphorically extended to nonphysical objects such as pieces of program.

DO PROTOCOL *verb.*

To perform an interaction with somebody or something according to a well-defined standard procedure. For example: "Let's do protocol with the check" at a restaurant means to ask the waitress for the check, calculate the tip and everybody's share, make change as necessary, and pay the bill.

DOUBLE BUCKY *adjective.*

Using both the *"control"* and *"meta"* keys on a keyboard that has them. "The EMACS command to reformat a LISP program is double-bucky-G." (That is, the command is control-meta-G.)

For a complete explanation, see BUCKY BITS.

The following lyrics were written on May 27, 1978, in cele-

bration of the Stanford keyboard. A typical MIT comment was
that the "bucky bits" ("control" and "meta" shifting keys) were
nice, but there weren't enough of them—you could only type
512 different characters on a Stanford keyboard. An obvious
thing was simply to add more shifting keys, and this was eventually done. One problem is that a keyboard with that many
shifting keys is hard on touch typists, who don't like to move
their hands away from the home position on the keyboard. It
was half-seriously suggested that the extra shifting keys be
pedals; typing on such a keyboard would be very much like
playing a pipe organ. This idea is mentioned below, in what is
a parody of a very fine song by Jeffrey Moss called "Rubber
Duckie," which was published in *The Sesame Street Songbook.*

Double Bucky

Double bucky, you're the one!
You make my keyboard lots of fun.
    Double bucky, an additional bit or two:
(Vo-vo-de-o!)
Control and meta, side by side.
Augmented ASCII, nine bits wide!
    Double bucky! Half a thousand glyphs, plus a few!
        Oh,
        I sure wish that I
        Had a couple of
            Bits more!
        Perhaps a
        Set of pedals to
        Make the number of
            Bits four:
        Double double bucky!
Double bucky, left and right
OR'd together, outta sight!
    Double bucky, I'd like a whole word of
    Double bucky, I'm happy I heard of
    Double bucky, I'd like a whole word of you!

                        –The Great QUUX
                (with apologies to Jeffrey Moss)

DOWN *adjective*

Not working; deactivated. Example: "The Up escalator is down." That is considered a humorous thing to say, but "The elevator is down" *always* means "The elevator isn't working," and never refers to what floor the elevator is on.

Antonym: UP.

GO DOWN *verb.* To stop functioning, usually said of the SYSTEM. The message every hacker hates to hear from the operator is, "The system will go down in five minutes."

TAKE DOWN, BRING DOWN *verb.* To deactivate purposely, usually for repair work. Example: "I'm taking the system down to work on that BUG in the tape drive."

See CRASH.

DPB *(d:-pib', duh-pib')* *verb.*

To plop something down in the middle. *Silly.* Example: "Dpb yourself into that couch there." (The connotation would be that the couch is full except for one slot just big enough for you to sit in. DPB means "DePosit Byte," and is the name of a PDP-10 instruction that inserts some BITS into the middle of some other bits.)

DRAGON *noun.*

A program similar to a DAEMON, except that it doesn't sit around waiting for something to happen but is instead used by the SYSTEM to perform various useful tasks that just have to be done periodically.

A typical example would be an accounting program that accumulates statistics, keeps track of who is logged in, and so on.

Another example: Most time-sharing systems have several terminals, and at any given time some are in use and some are sitting idle. The idle ones usually sit there with some idiotic message on their screens, such as "logged off," from the last time someone used it. One time-sharing system at MIT puts these idle terminals to good use by displaying useful information on them, such as who is using the computer, where they are, what they're doing, and what their telephone numbers are, along with other information such as pretty pictures (the picture collection includes a unicorn, Snoopy, and the U.S.S. *Enterprise* from "Star Trek"). All this information is displayed on idle terminals by the "name dragon," so called because it originally printed just the names of the users. (That it now shows all kinds of things, including useless though pretty pictures, is an example of CREEPING FEATURISM.) The "name dragon" is a program started up by the system, and it runs about every five minutes and updates the information on all idle terminals.

DWIM *(dwim) noun.*
A complicated procedure (in the INTERLISP dialect of LISP) that attempts to correct your mistakes automatically. For example, if you spell something wrong or don't balance your parentheses properly, it tries to figure out what you meant. DWIM stands for "Do What I Mean." When this works, it is very impressive. When it doesn't work, anything can happen.

When a program has become very big and complicated—so complicated that no one can understand how to use it—it is often suggested in jest that dwim be added to it.

See BELLS AND WHISTLES.

EL CAMINO BIGNUM *(el' k:-mee'noh big'num) noun.*
El Camino Real.
El Camino Real is the name of a street through the San Francisco peninsula that originally extended (and still appears in places) all the way down to Mexico City. Navigation on the San Francisco peninsula is usually done relative to El Camino Real, which is assumed to run north and south even though it doesn't really in many places (see LOGICAL). El Camino Real runs right past Stanford University, and so is familiar to hackers.

The Spanish word *real,* which has two syllables *(ree-ahl'),* means "royal"; El Camino Real is "the royal road." Now, the English word *real* is used in mathematics to describe numbers (and by analogy is misused in computer jargon to mean floating-point numbers). In the FORTRAN language, for example, a "real" quantity is a number typically precise to seven decimal places; and a "double-precision" quantity is a larger floating-

point number, precise to perhaps fourteen decimal places.
When a hacker from MIT visited Stanford in 1976 or so, he
remarked what a long road El Camino Real was. Making a pun
on "real," he started calling it "El Camino Double Precision."
But when the hacker was told that the road was hundreds of
miles long, he renamed it "El Camino Bignum," and among
hackers that name has stuck. (See BIGNUM.)

ENGLISH *noun.*
The source code for a program, which may be in any computer
language.

This term is slightly obsolete, and used mostly by old-time
hackers who were around MIT in the mid-1960s. To a real
hacker, a program written in his favorite programming language is as readable as English.

EPSILON *(ep'si-lahn)*
1. *noun.* A small quantity of anything. Example: The "cost is
   epsilon."
2. *adjective.* Very small, negligible. "I tried to speed up the
   program, but got epsilon improvement."

WITHIN EPSILON OF *preposition.* Close enough to be indistinguishable for all practical purposes. This is even closer than
being within DELTA of. Example: "That's not what I asked for,
but it's within epsilon of what I wanted." Alternatively, it may
mean *not* close enough, but very little is required to get it
there: "My program is within epsilon of working."

EPSILON SQUARED *noun.* A quantity even smaller than
epsilon, as small in relation to epsilon as epsilon is to something
normal. Suppose you buy a large computer for one million
dollars. You probably need a thousand-dollar terminal to go
with it, but by comparison the cost of that is epsilon. If you need
a ten-dollar cable to connect them together, its cost is epsilon
squared.

See DELTA.

The terms *epsilon* and *delta* are names of Greek letters; the
slang usage stems from the traditional use of these letters in
mathematics for very small numerical quantities, particularly
in so-called "epsilon-delta" proofs in the differential calculus.

Once "epsilon" has been mentioned, "delta" is usually used to mean a quantity that is slightly greater than epsilon but still very small. For example, "The cost isn't epsilon, but it's delta" means that the cost isn't totally negligible, but it is nevertheless very small. A quantity that is a little bit smaller than epsilon is "epsilon over 2," and "epsilon squared" is very much smaller than epsilon.

EXCH *(eks′ch:, ekstch) verb.*
To exchange two things, one for the other; to swap places. *Silly.* If you point to two people sitting down and say, "Exch!" you are asking them to trade places.

EXCH, meaning EXCHange, is the name of a PDP-10 instruction that exchanges the contents of a register and a memory location.

EXCL *(eks′c:l) noun.*
The character "!". See CHARACTERS.

FAULTY *adjective.*
Nonfunctional; buggy.

This word means about the same thing as BAGBITING, BLETCHEROUS, and LOSING, but the connotation is much milder.

FEATURE *noun.*
1. An intended property or behavior (as of a program). Whether it is good is immaterial.
2. A good property or behavior (as of a program). Whether it was intended is immaterial.
3. A surprising property or behavior; in particular, one that is purposely inconsistent because it works better that way. For example, in the EMACS text editor, the "transpose characters" command will exchange the two characters on either side of the cursor on the screen, *except* when the cursor is at the end of a line; in that case, the two characters before the cursor are exchanged. While this behavior is perhaps surprising, and certainly inconsistent, it has been found through extensive experimentation to be what most users want. The inconsistency is therefore a feature and not a BUG.

4. A property or behavior that is gratuitous or unnecessary, though perhaps impressive or cute. For example, one feature of the MACLISP language is the ability to print numbers as Roman numerals. See BELLS AND WHISTLES.
5. A property or behavior that was put in to help someone else but that happens to be in your way. A standard joke is that a bug can be turned into a feature simply by documenting it (then theoretically no one can complain about it because it's in the manual), or even by simply declaring it to be good. "That's not a bug; it's a feature!"

If someone tells you about some new improvement to a program, you might respond, "Feetch, feetch!" The meaning of this depends critically on vocal inflection. With enthusiasm, it means something like "Boy, that's great! What a great HACK!" Grudgingly or with obvious doubt, it means "I don't know. It sounds like just one more unnecessary and complicated thing." With a tone of resignation, it means "Well, I'd rather keep it simple, but I suppose it has to be done."

The following list covers the spectrum of terms used to rate programs or portions thereof (except for the first two, which tend to be applied more to hardware or to the SYSTEM, but are included for completeness):

CRASH	LOSS	HACK
STOPPAGE	MISFEATURE	WIN
BRAIN DAMAGE	CROCK	FEATURE
BUG	KLUGE	PERFECTION

The last is never actually attained.

FEEP *(feep)*
1. *noun.* The soft electronic "bell" of a display terminal (except for a DEC VT-52!): a beep.
2. *verb.* To make (or to cause a terminal to make) a "feep" sound.
FEEPER *noun.* The device in the terminal (usually a loudspeaker of some kind) that makes the feep sound.

FEEPING CREATURISM *noun.* This term isn't really well defined, but it sounds so nice (being a spoonerism on CREEPING FEATURISM) that most hackers have said or heard it. It probably has something to do with terminals prowling about in the dark making their customary noises.

A true TTY does not feep; it has a real mechanical bell that just rings. Synonyms for "feep" are "beep," "bleep," or just about anything suitably onomatopoeic. (Jeff MacNelly, in his comic strip *Shoe*, uses the word "eep" for sounds made by computer terminals and video games; this is perhaps the closest one yet.) The term "breedle" is sometimes heard at Stanford, where the terminal bleepers are not particularly soft. (They sound more like the musical equivalent of a raspberry or a Bronx cheer. For a close approximation, imagine the sound of a "Star Trek" communicator's beep lasting for five seconds.) By contrast, the feeper on a DEC VT-52 terminal has been compared to the sound of a '52 Chevy stripping its gears.

FENCEPOST ERROR *noun.*
An "off-by-one" error: the discrete equivalent of a boundary condition.

This problem is often exhibited in programs containing iterative loops: something will be done one time too few or too many. The term comes from the following problem: "If you build a fence 100 feet long with posts 10 feet apart, how many posts do you need?" (Either 9 or 11 is a better answer than the obvious 10.)

For example, suppose you have a long list or array of items and want to process items m through n. How many items are there? The obvious answer is $n - m$, but that is off by one. The right answer is $n - m + 1$. A program that used the "obvious" formula would have a fencepost error in it.

Not all off-by-one problems are fencepost errors. The game of Musical Chairs involves an off-by-one problem where N people try to sit in $N - 1$ chairs, but it's not a fencepost error. A fencepost error is typified by counting things rather than counting the spaces between them, or vice versa, or by neg-

lecting to consider whether one should count one or both of the
ends of a row.

FINE *adjective.*
Good, but not good enough to be CUSPY.

This term is used primarily at WPI. The word "fine" is occasionally heard elsewhere, too, but does not connote the implicit comparison to the higher level of perfection implied by
CUSPY.

FLAG *noun.*
A variable or quantity that can take on one of two values: a BIT,
particularly one that is used to indicate one of two outcomes
or is used to control which of two things is to be done. Examples: "This flag controls whether to clear the screen before
printing the message." "The program status word contains several flag bits."

FLAG DAY *noun.*
A day on which a change is made that is neither forward- nor
backward-compatible (so old programs won't work under the
new system, and new programs won't work under the old one),
and that is costly to make and costly to undo. Example: "If we
change MACLISP to use square brackets instead of parentheses, it will cause a flag day for everybody." A flag day, as well
as the weeks or months following, is a time of great confusion
for everyone concerned.

This term has nothing to do with the use of the word FLAG
to mean a variable that has two values. It came into use when
a massive change was made to the MULTICS time-sharing
system to convert from the old ASCII code to the new one. This
was scheduled for Flag Day, June 14, 1966.

FLAKY, FLAKEY *adjective.*
Subject to frequent or intermittent failure.

This use is of course related to the common slang use of the
word, to describe a person as eccentric or crazy. A system that
is flakey is working, sort of, enough that you are tempted to try
to use it; but it fails frequently enough that the odds in favor
of finishing what you start are low.

FLAME

1. *verb.* To speak incessantly and/or rabidly on some relatively uninteresting subject or with a patently ridiculous attitude.
2. *noun.* A speech or dialogue in which the speakers are flaming.
3. *noun.* A subject on which a given person likes to flame.

    FLAME SESSION *noun.* A meeting in which everyone flames; a "bull session."

    FLAME ON *verb.* To continue to flame.

    FLAMER *noun.* One who flames: a fanatic.

    FLAMAGE *(flaym':j) noun.* Flaming; the content of a flame. (Both flamage and flaming are used in this sense.)

    Synonym: RAVE.

    When a discussion degenerates into useless controversy, one might tell the participants, "Now you're just flaming!" or "Stop all that flamage!" to get them to cool down (so to speak).

FLAP *verb.*

To give the command to unload a MICROTAPE or, more generally, any magnetic tape from its drive. (When this operation is finished, the take-up reel keeps spinning and the end of the tape goes flap, flap, flap. . . .) "I need to use the tape drive; could you please flap your tape?"

FLAVOR *noun.*

1. Variety, type, kind. "EMACS commands come in two flavors: single-character and named." "These lights come in two flavors: big red ones and small green ones." See VANILLA.
2. The attribute that causes something to be FLAVORFUL. Usually used in the phrase "yields additional flavor." Example: "This feature yields additional flavor by allowing one to print text either right-side-up or upside down."

    FLAVORFUL *adjective.* Aesthetically pleasing. Antonym: BLETCHEROUS. See TASTE.

FLUSH *verb.*

1. To delete, destroy, or get rid of something, typically something that is useless or superfluous. "All that nonsense has

been flushed." This is standard MIT terminology within the ITS time-sharing SYSTEM for aborting an output operation. One speaks of the text that would have been printed—but was not—as having been "flushed." Under that time-sharing system, if you ask to have a file printed on your terminal, it is printed a page at a time; at the end of each page, it asks whether you want to see more. If you say no, it says "FLUSHED." (A speculation is that this term arose from a vivid image of flushing unwanted characters by hosing down the internal output buffer, washing the characters away before they can be printed.)

2. To exclude someone from an activity.
3. To leave at the end of a day's work (as opposed to leaving for a meal). Examples: "I'm going to flush now." "Time to flush." see GRONK OUT.

FOO *(foo)*

1. *interjection.* Term of disgust. For greater emphasis, one says MOBY FOO (see MOBY).
2. *noun.* The first metasyntactic variable. When you have to invent an arbitrary temporary name for something for the sake of exposition, FOO is usually used. If you need a second one, BAR or BAZ is usually used; there is a slight preference at MIT for bar and at Stanford for baz. (It was probably at Stanford that bar was corrupted to baz. Clearly, bar was the original, for the concatenation FOOBAR is widely used also, and this in turn can be traced to the obscene acronym "FUBAR" that arose in the armed forces during World War II.) If bar is used, then baz is used as a third name, and QUUX enjoys some popularity as the next name after that.

   Example: "The bug can happen in this way. Suppose you have two functions FOO and BAR. FOO calls BAR with two arguments. Now BAR calls BAZ, passing it just one of the two arguments . . ." In effect, these words serve as extra pronouns; they are always "nonce names." The very fact that they always serve this purpose allows some abbreviation. The preceding example might be shortened without loss of clarity to: "The bug can happen in this way. Suppose

FOO calls BAR with two arguments. Now BAR calls BAZ, passing it just one of the two arguments . . ."

Words such as "foo" are called "metasyntactic variables" because, just as a mathematical variable stands for some number, so "foo" always stands for the real name of the thing under discussion. A hacker avoids using "foo" as the real name of anything. Indeed, a standard convention is that any file with "foo" in its name is temporary and can be deleted on sight.

FOO? What? What's going on here? See COM MODE.

FOOBAR A concatenation of FOO and BAR.

"Foo" is certainly a favorite among hackers. While its use in connection with BAR clearly stems from "FUBAR," its original appearance appears to be untraceable, and may derive from other common interjections such as the Yiddish "Feh!." Bill Holman featured the word "foo" prominently in his comic strip *Smokey Stover*.

FRIED *adjective*.

1. Nonfunctional because of hardware failure; burned out. Example: "The disk controller is fried." (Sometimes this literally happens to electronic circuits! In particular, resistors can burn out and transformers can melt down, emitting terrible-smelling smoke. However, this term is also used metaphorically.)

2. Of people, exhausted, "burned out." This is said particularly of those who continue to work in such a state, and often used as an explanation or excuse. Example: "Yeah, I know that fix destroyed the file system, but I was fried when I put it in."

See FRY.

FROB *(frahb)*

1. *noun*. A protruding arm or trunnion. (This is the official definition by the Tech Model Railroad Club at MIT.)

2. Any somewhat small thing; an object that you can comfortably hold in one hand. Something you can frob. See FROBNICATE.

3. *verb*. Abbreviated form of FROBNICATE.

FROBNICATE *(frahb'ni-kayt) verb.* To manipulate or adjust; to do the appropriate thing to; to play with; to fondle. This word is usually abbreviated to simply "frob," but frobnicate is recognized as the official full form. Examples: "Please frob the light switch." (That is, flip the light switch.) "Stop frobbing that clasp. You'll break it."

Synonyms: TWEAK, TWIDDLE.

Frob, twiddle, and tweak sometimes connote points along a spectrum. Frob connotes aimless manipulation; twiddle connotes gross manipulation, often a coarse search for a proper setting; tweak connotes fine tuning. Suppose someone is turning a knob on an oscilloscope. If he's carefully adjusting it, searching for some particular point, he is probably tweaking it. If he is turning it rather quickly while looking at the screen, he is probably twiddling it. But if he's just doing it because turning a knob is fun, he's frobbing it.

FROBNITZ *(frahb'nitz), plural* **FROBNITZEM** *(frahb'nit-z:m) noun.*

1. An unspecified physical object; a widget; a black box.
2. By extension, a data structure in a program, when regarded as an object.

   This rare form is usually abbreviated to FROTZ *(frahtz)*, or more commonly, to FROB. Also used are frobnule *(frahb' nyool)*, frobule *(frahb'yool)*, and frobnodule *(frahb-nahd' yool)*. Starting perhaps in 1979, "frobboz" *(fruh-bahz', fr: -bahz')*, plural "frobbotzim" *(fruh-baht'z:m)*, has also become very popular, largely due to its exposure as a name via the Adventure-type game called Zork (which originated at MIT).

FROG, PHROG

1. *interjection.* Term of disgust. (Hackers seem to have a lot of them.)
2. *noun.* Of things, a CROCK. Of people, something between a turkey and a toad.

   FROGGY *adjective.* Similar to BAGBITING, but milder. "This froggy program is taking forever to run!"

FROTZ *(frahtz) noun.*
An abbreviated form of FROBNITZ.

MUMBLE FROTZ *interjection.* A term of fairly mild disgust, usually used as an objection to something someone has just said. See MUMBLE.

FRY *verb.*
1. To fail. Said especially of smoke-producing hardware failures.
2. More generally, to become nonworking. (This term is never said of software, only of hardware and humans.)
   See FRIED.

FTP *(ef' tee' pee')*
1. *noun.* The File Transfer Protocol for transmitting files between systems on the ARPANET.
2. *noun.* A program that implements the protocol and thereby helps you to transfer files.
3. *verb.* To transfer a file using the File Transfer Program. Example: "Lemme get this copy of *Wuthering Heights* FTP'd from Stanford."
4. *verb.* More generally, to transfer a file between two computers using any electronic network such as ETHERNET (as opposed, say, to using a magnetic tape as the transfer medium).

FUDGE
1. *verb.* To perform in an incomplete but marginally acceptable way, particularly with respect to the writing of a program. "I didn't feel like doing it all the right way, so I fudged it."
2. *noun.* The code resulting from fudging as defined above.
3. *verb.* To make something come out the way it was supposed to by making an *ex post facto* change, such as to a FUDGE FACTOR.
   All these uses are related to the common slang use of the word to mean something like cheating, as when a scientist fudges his measurements to fit his pet theory.

FUDGE FACTOR *noun.* A value or parameter that is varied in an *ad hoc* way to produce a desired result. See SLOP.

GABRIEL *noun.*
An unnecessary (in the opinion of the opponent) stalling tactic when playing volleyball, such as tying one's shoelaces repeatedly or asking the time. Also used to refer to the perpetrator of such tactics.

GABRIEL MODE *noun.* The state a person is in when he performs one stalling tactic after another. See MODE.

This is in honor of Richard P. Gabriel, a Stanford hacker and volleyball fanatic. His reputation for stalling is a bit undeserved, and has the status of a running gag. One may speak of "pulling a Gabriel" or of "being in Gabriel mode."

See RPG.

GARPLY *(gahrp'lee) noun.*
A meta-word, like FOO. This one is used mostly at Stanford.

GAS
1. *interjection.* A term of disgust and hatred, implying that gas should be dispensed in generous quantities, thereby exterminating the source of irritation. "Some LOSER just reloaded the SYSTEM for no reason! Gas!"
2. An exclamation suggesting that someone or something ought to be FLUSHED (gotten rid of) out of mercy. "The system is getting WEDGED every few minutes. Gas!"
3. *verb.* To get rid of; to flush. "You should gas that old CRUFTY software."

GASEOUS *adjective.* Deserving of being gassed.

GC *(jee'see')*
1. *verb.* To clean up and throw away useless things. "I think I'll GC the top of my desk today."
2. To recycle, reclaim, or put to another use.
3. To forget. (The implication is sometimes that one has done so deliberately.) "You told me last week where it was, but I GC'd those bits."
4. *noun.* An instantiation of the GC process.

GC is an abbreviation of "garbage collect" or "garbage

collection," which is computer science jargon for a particular class of strategies used to recycle computer memory. One such strategy involves periodically scanning all the data in memory and discarding useless data items.

Occasionally the full phrase is used. Note the ambiguity in usage which has to be resolved by context: "I'm going to garbage-collect my desk" usually means to clean out the drawers, but it could also mean to throw away or recycle the desk itself.

GEDANKEN *(ge-dahnk-:n) adjective.*
Wild-eyed; impractical; not well-thought-out; untried; untested.

Gedanken is a German word for *thought.* A thought experiment is one you carry out in your head. In physics, the term "gedanken experiment" refers to an experiment that is impractical to carry out but useful to consider theoretically. (A classic gedanken experiment of relativity theory involves thinking about a man flying through space in an elevator.) Gedanken experiments are very useful in physics, but you have to be careful. It was a gedanken experiment that led Aristotle to conclude that heavy things always fall faster than light things (he thought about a rock and a feather). This was accepted until Galileo proved otherwise.

Among hackers, however, the word has a pejorative connotation. It is said of a project—especially one in artificial intelligence research—which is written up in grand detail (typically as a Ph.D. thesis) without ever being implemented to any great extent. Such a project is usually perpetrated by people who aren't very good hackers or find programming distasteful or are just in a hurry. A gedanken thesis is usually marked by an obvious lack of intuition about what is programmable and what is not, and about what does and does not constitute a clear specification of an algorithm.

GLASS TTY *(glass ti'tee) noun.*
A terminal which has a display screen but which, because of hardware or software limitations, behaves like a teletype or

other printing terminal, thereby combining the disadvantages of both. Like a printing terminal, it can't do fancy display hacks; and like a display terminal, it doesn't produce hard copy (a paper copy that you can carry away with you). An example is the Lear Siegler ADM-3 terminal, which was actually advertised as "the dumb terminal" when it first came out (implying that it was also cheap). See TTY.

GLITCH

1. *noun.* A sudden interruption in electric service, sanity, continuity, or program function. It may or may not be possible to recover from it.
2. *verb.* To commit a glitch. See GRITCH.

An interruption in electric service is usually called a "power glitch." This is of grave concern because it usually CRASHES all the computers.

Have you ever been in the middle of a sentence and then forgotten what you were going to say? If this happened to a hacker, he might say, "Sorry, I just glitched." (This would be a "mental glitch.")

This word almost certainly comes from Yiddish, where the verb *glitschen* means to slide or skid on a slippery surface. A fall while walking on ice would be a *glitch.*

3. *verb.* To scroll a display screen.

The use of "glitch" to mean "scroll" needs some explanation. When a program prints text on a display screen, there is a question of what to do when it reaches the last line of the screen. There are two main strategies:

After the last line, go back to the top line (possibly clearing the screen first). This is called "wraparound."

Move all the lines of text on the screen upward one line. The top line of text disappears (it "falls off the top of the screen") because there's no more room for it, and the bottom line of the screen becomes empty and can be used to display the next line of text. This is called "scrolling," because it looks as though a papyrus scroll is zipping past your eyes, unwinding at the bottom and winding up again at the top.

The advantage of the scrolling technique is that new text always appears at the bottom of the screen. The disadvantage is that all the text keeps moving upward as new lines are displayed, so it's awfully hard to read it as it flashes by on the screen. (Movie fans know about this problem from trying to read the credits at the end.)

The computer system at Stanford compromises. It scrolls, but when the last line of the screen has been used, the text is moved up many lines (about ten or so). This means that the top ten lines all disappear at once, but the rest stay put on the screen while the next ten lines are being displayed at the bottom. So instead of appearing to move continuously up the screen, the text "jerks" or "glitches" every five seconds or so.

GLORK *(glohrk)*

1. *interjection.* Term of mild surprise, usually tinged with outrage, as when one attempts to save the results of two hours of editing and finds that the SYSTEM has just CRASHED.
2. A meta-word. See FOO.
3. *verb.* Similar to GLITCH, but usually used reflexively. "My program just glorked itself."

GOBBLE *verb.*

To consume or to obtain. "Gobble up" tends to imply "consume," while "gobble down" tends to imply "obtain."

Examples: "The output spy gobbles characters out of a TTY output buffer." (See OUTPUT SPY.) "I guess I'll gobble down a copy of the documentation tomorrow."

See SNARF.

GORP *(gohrp)*

This is yet another metasyntactic variable like FOO and BAR. It is used primarily at CMU. (It may be related to its use as the generic term for hiker's dried food, stemming from the acronym "Good Old Raisins and Peanuts," but this is uncertain.)

GOSPERISM *(gahss'p:r-iz':m)*

A hack, invention, or saying by arch-hacker R. William (Bill) Gosper. This notion merits its own term because there are so many of them. Many of the entries in HAKMEM are gosperisms. See also LIFE.

GRIND *verb.*

1. To format code, especially LISP code, by indenting the lines so that it looks pretty. (This term is used primarily within the MACLISP community. Elsewhere, to format code so that it looks nice is to "pretty-print" it.)
2. To run seemingly interminably, performing some tedious and inherently useless task. Synonym: CRUNCH.

GRITCH

1. *noun.* A complaint (often caused by a GLITCH).
2. *verb.* To complain. Often verb-doubled: "Gritch, gritch."

GROK *(grahk) verb.*

To understand, usually in a global sense; especially, to understand all the implications and consequences of making a change. Example: "JONL is the only one who groks the MACLISP compiler."

This word comes from the science-fiction novel *Stranger in a Strange Land* by Robert Heinlein, where it is a Martian word meaning roughly "to be one with."

GRONK *(grahnk) verb.*

To clear the state of a WEDGED device and restart it. More severe than "to FROB."

GRONKED *adjective.* Of people, the condition of feeling very tired or sick. Of things, totally nonfunctional. (For things, gronked and BROKEN mean about the same thing, but they have very different connotations when used of people. "Gronked" connotes physical exhaustion or illness, while "broken" connotes mental or emotional illness.)

GRONK OUT *verb.* Of things, to cease functioning. "My terminal just gronked out." Of people, to go home and go to sleep. "I guess I'll gronk out now. See you all tomorrow." When you are gronked, the best thing to do is to gronk out.

"Gronk out" is a more specific term than "flush." In both cases you stop hacking and leave, but when you flush you might go home or might go to a restaurant or to see a movie. If you gronk out, however, you intend to go get some sleep.

GRONK has been popularized as a noise made by dinosaurs in the comic strip *B.C.*, by Johnny Hart, but the hackers' connotation apparently predates Hart's usage.

GROVEL *verb.*

1. To work interminably and without apparent progress. Often used with "over" or "through." Example: "The file scavenger has been groveling through the file directories for ten minutes now."
2. To examine minutely or in complete detail. "The compiler grovels over the entire source program before beginning to translate it." "I groveled through all the documentation, but I still couldn't find the command I wanted."

   GROVEL OBSCENELY. This is the standard emphatic form of grovel.

GRUNGY *(gruhn'jee) adjective.*

1. Incredibly dirty, greasy, grubby. Anything that has been washed within the last year is not really grungy. If you sleep all night in your clothes and then get up and start hacking again, you feel grungy.
2. More generally, awful or ugly. Programs (especially CROCKS) can be described as grungy. A person with a headache or a cold probably feels grungy.

GUBBISH *(guhb'ish) noun.*

Garbage; crap; nonsense. "What is all this gubbish?" (This word is probably a portmanteau of "garbage" and "rubbish.")

GUN *verb.*

To forcibly terminate a program. May be used with or without "down." "Some idiot left a useless background program running, soaking up half the CYCLES. So I gunned it."

HACK

1. *noun.* A quick bit of work that produces what is needed, but not well.
2. The result of that work: a CROCK. (Occasionally the connotation is affectionate.)

3. An incredibly good, and perhaps very time-consuming, piece of work that produces exactly what is needed.
4. The result of that work.
5. A clever technique.
6. A brilliant practical joke. The value of the hack varies in proportion to its cleverness, harmlessness, surprise value, fame, and appropriate use of technology.
7. *verb.* With "together," to throw something together so it will work. See CRUFT and KLUDGE.
8. To bear something emotionally or physically. "I can't hack this heat!"
9. To work with a computer.
10. To work on something (typically a program). In specific sense: "What are you doing?" "I'm hacking TECO." In general sense: "What do you do around here?" "I hack TECO." (The former is time-immediate, the latter time-extended.) More generally, "I hack x" is roughly equivalent to "X is my bag." Example: "I hack solid-state physics."
11. To pull a prank on. See definition 6 above, and also definition 7 of HACKER.
12. To waste time (as opposed to TOOL). Example: "Watcha up to?" "Oh, just hacking."

HACK VALUE *noun.* Term used as the reason or motivation for expending effort toward a seemingly useless goal, the point being that the accomplished goal is a hack. For example, the MACLISP language can read and print integers as Roman numerals; the code for this was installed purely for hack value.

HACK UP (ON) *verb.* To hack, but with the connotation that the result is a hack as in definition 2, above. Examples: "You need a quick-and-dirty sorting routine? I'll see if I can hack one up by tomorrow." "I hacked up on EMACS so it can use the Greek alphabet."

HOW'S HACKING? A friendly greeting among hackers. (It recognizes the other person as a hacker and invites him to describe what he has been working on recently.)

HAPPY HACKING A farewell.

BACK TO HACKING Another farewell. "Happy hacking" implies that the other person will continue hacking (perhaps you interrupted him). "Oh, well, back to hacking" implies that you, the speaker, are going to return to work (and perhaps the other person also).

HACK, HACK A somewhat pointless but friendly comment, often used as a farewell but occasionally also as a greeting.

"The word 'hack' doesn't really have sixty-nine different meanings," according to Phil Agre, an MIT hacker. "In fact, 'hack' has only one meaning, an extremely subtle and profound one which defies articulation. Which connotation is implied by a given use of the word depends in similarly profound ways on the context. Similar remarks apply to a couple of other hacker words, most notably RANDOM."

Hacking might be characterized as "an appropriate application of ingenuity." Whether the result is a quick-and-dirty patchwork job or a carefully crafted work of art, you have to admire the cleverness that went into it. Here are examples of practical-joke hacks:

(1) In 1961, students from Caltech (California Institute of Technology in Pasadena) hacked the Rose Bowl football game. One student posed as a reporter and "interviewed" the director of the University of Washington card stunts (such stunts involve people in the stands who hold up colored cards to make pictures). The reporter learned exactly how the stunts were operated, and also that the director would be out to dinner later.

While the director was eating, the students (who called themselves the "Fiendish Fourteen") picked a lock and stole one of the direction sheets for the card stunts. They then had a printer run off 2300 copies of the sheet. The next day they picked the lock again and stole the master plans for the stunts, large sheets of graph paper colored in with the stunt pictures. Using these as a guide, they carefully made "corrections" for three of the stunts on the duplicate instruction sheets. Finally, they broke in once more, replacing the stolen master plans and substituting the stack of altered instruction sheets for the original set. The result was that three of the pictures were totally different. Instead of spelling WASHINGTON, the word CAL-

TECH was flashed. Another stunt showed the word HUSKIES, the Washington nickname, but spelled it backward. And what was supposed to have been a picture of a husky instead showed a beaver. (Both Caltech and MIT use the beaver as a mascot. Beavers are nature's engineers.)

After the game, the Washington faculty athletic representative said, "Some thought it ingenious; others were indignant." The Washington student body president remarked, "No hard feelings, but at the time it was unbelievable. We were amazed."

This is now considered a classic hack, particularly because revising the direction sheets constituted a form of programming not unlike computer programming.

(2) On November 20, 1982, MIT hacked the Harvard-Yale football game. Just after Harvard's second touchdown against Yale in the second quarter, a small black ball popped up out of the ground at the 40-yard line and grew bigger and bigger and bigger. The letters "MIT" appeared all over the ball. As the players and officials stood around gawking, the ball grew to six feet in diameter and then burst with a bang and a cloud of white smoke.

As the Boston *Globe* later reported, "If you want to know the truth, MIT won The Game."

The prank had taken weeks of careful planning by members of MIT's Delta Kappa Epsilon fraternity. The device consisted of a weather balloon, a hydraulic ram powered by Freon gas to lift it out of the ground, and a vacuum-cleaner motor to inflate it. The hackers made eight separate expeditions to Harvard Stadium between 1:00 and 5:00 A.M., in which they located an unused 110-volt circuit in the stadium and ran buried wiring from the stadium circuit to the 40-yard line, where they buried the balloon device. When the time came to activate the device, two fraternity members had merely to flip a circuit breaker and push a plug into an outlet.

This stunt had all the earmarks of a perfect hack: surprise, publicity, the ingenious use of technology, safety, and harmlessness. The use of manual control allowed the prank to be

timed so as not to disrupt the game (it was set off between plays
so the outcome of the game would not be affected). The perpe-
trators had even thoughtfully attached a note to the balloon
explaining that the device was not dangerous and contained no
explosives.

Harvard president Derek Bok commented: "They have an
awful lot of clever people down there at MIT, and they did
it again." President Paul E. Gray of MIT said, "There is
absolutely no truth to the rumor that I had anything to do
with it, but I wish there were." Such is the way of all good
hacks.

HACK ATTACK *noun.*
A period of greatly increased hacking activity. "I've been up
for thirty hours; I had a hack attack and finished off that new
FEATURE I thought would take two weeks to program."

HACKER *noun.*
1. A person who enjoys learning the details of computer systems and how to stretch their capabilities—as opposed to
   most users of computers, who prefer to learn only the minimum amount necessary.
2. One who programs enthusiastically, or who enjoys programming rather than just theorizing about programming.
3. A person capable of appreciating HACK VALUE.
4. A person who is good at programming quickly. (By the way,
   not everything a hacker produces is a hack.)
5. An expert on a particular program, or one who frequently
   does work using it or on it. Example: "A SAIL hacker." (This
   definition and the preceding ones are correlated, and people
   who fit them congregate.)
6. An expert of any kind. One might be an astronomy hacker,
   for example.
7. A malicious or inquisitive meddler who tries to discover
   information by poking around. For example, a "password
   hacker" is one who tries, possibly by deceptive or illegal
   means, to discover other people's computer passwords. A
   "network hacker" is one who tries to learn about the com-

puter network (possibly because he wants to improve it or possibly because he wants to interfere—one can tell the difference only by context and tone of voice).

HACKISH *adjective.* Being or involving a hack.

HACKISHNESS, HACKITUDE *noun.* The quality of being or involving a hack. (The word "hackitude" is considered silly; the standard term is "hackishness.")

Hackers consider themselves somewhat of an elite, though one to which new members are gladly welcome. It is a meritocracy based on ability. There is a certain self-satisfaction in identifying yourself as a hacker (but if you claim to be one and are not, you're quickly labeled BOGUS).

HAIR *noun.*

Complexity. "Decoding TECO commands requires a certain amount of hair."

INFINITE HAIR, HAIR SQUARED *noun.* Extreme complexity. The phrase "infinite hair" is usually used in sentences, while "hair squared" is used as an interjection. For example: "I wrote a program to do my income taxes; properly handling Schedule G required infinite hair." (To which his friend replies, "Hair squared!")

HAIRY *adjective.*
1. Overly complicated. "DWIM is incredibly hairy."
2. Incomprehensible. "DWIM is incredibly hairy."
3. Of people: High-powered, authoritative, rare, expert, or incomprehensible. This usage is difficult to explain except by example: "He knows a hairy lawyer who says there's nothing to worry about." F. Lee Bailey would be considered hairy.

HAKMEM *(hak'mem) noun.*

MIT Artificial Intelligence Memo 239 (February 1972). A collection of neat mathematical, programming, and electronic hacks contributed by people at MIT and elsewhere. (The title of the memo really is HAKMEM, which is a portmanteau word for "hacks memo.") Some of them are very useful techniques or powerful theorems, but most fall into the category of mathematical and computer trivia. A sampling of the entries (with authors), slightly paraphrased:

Item 41.   (Gene Salamin) There are exactly 23,000 prime numbers less than 2^{18}.

Item 46.   (Rich Schroeppel) The most *probable* suit distribution in bridge hands is 4-4-3-2, as compared to 4-3-3-3, which is the most *evenly* distributed. This is because the world likes to have unequal numbers: a thermodynamic effect saying things will not be in the state of lowest energy, but in the state of lowest disordered energy.

Problem 81.   (Rich Schroeppel) Count the magic squares of order 5 (that is, all the 5-by-5 arrangements of the numbers from 1 to 25 such that all rows, columns, and diagonals add up to the same number). There are about 320 million, not counting those that differ only by rotation and reflection.

Item 174.   (Bill Gosper and Stuart Nelson) 21963283741 is the only number such that if you represent it on the PDP-10 as both an integer and a floating-point number, the bit patterns of the two representations are identical.

HAKMEM also contains some rather more complicated mathematical and technical items, but these examples show some of its fun flavor.

HANDWAVE

1. *verb.* To gloss over a complex point; to distract a listener; to support a (possibly actually valid) point with blatantly faulty logic. If someone starts a sentence with "Clearly . . ." or "Obviously . . ." or "It is self-evident that . . . ," you can be sure he is about to handwave.

The idea is that if you wave your hands at the right moment, the listener may be sufficiently distracted that he will not notice that what you have said is BOGUS. Alternatively, if a listener does object, you might try to dismiss the objection "with a wave of your hand."

2. *noun.* A specific act of handwaving.

The use of this word is often accompanied by gestures: both hands up, palms forward, swinging the hands in a vertical plane pivoting at the elbows and/or shoulders (depending on the magnitude of the handwave); alternatively, holding the forearms still while rotating the hands at the wrist to make them flutter. In context, the gestures alone can suffice as a remark. If a speaker makes an outrageous, unsupported assumption, you might simply wave your hands in this way as an accusation, more eloquent than words could express, that his logic is faulty.

HANG *verb.*

1. To wait for some event to occur; to hang around until something happens. Example: "The program prints out a menu and then hangs until you type a character."

2. To wait for some event that will never occur. "The system is hanging because the disk controller never sent the interrupt signal."

HUNG *adjective.* In the state of hanging. If you're hacking away at a terminal and suddenly the computer stops responding, you might yell across the hallway, "Is the system hung?" Synonym: WEDGED.

HARDWARILY *(hahrd-war':-lee) adverb.*

In a way pertaining to hardware. "The SYSTEM is hardwarily unreliable." Note: the adjective "hardwary" is *not* used. See SOFTWARILY.

HIRSUTE *adjective.*

This word is occasionally used humorously as a synonym for HAIRY.

HOOK *noun.*

An extraneous piece of software or hardware included in order to simplify later changes or to permit changes by a user. For instance, a PDP-10 program might execute a location that is normally a JFCL (no operation), but by changing the JFCL to a PUSHJ (subroutine call) one can insert a debugging routine at that point.

As another example, a simple program that prints numbers might always print them in base ten, but a more flexible version would let a variable determine what base to use. Setting the variable to "5" would make the program print numbers in base five. The variable is a simple hook. An even more flexible program might examine the variable and treat a value of sixteen or less as the base to use, but treat any other number as the address of a user-supplied program for printing a number. This is a very powerful hook: one can then write a routine to print numbers as Roman numerals, say, or as Hebrew characters, and connect it to the program by hanging it on the hook.

Often the difference between a good program and a superb one is that the latter has useful hooks in judiciously chosen places. Both may do the original job about equally well, but the one with the hooks is much more flexible for future expansion of capabilities.

ILL MEM REF *(ill'mem'ref')* *noun.*
A lapse of memory; a GLITCH. This phrase is a contraction of "illegal memory reference," computer jargon for the result of improperly accessing a computer's memory. Example: "I recognized his face, but got an ill mem ref on his name."
See NXM.

INFINITE *adjective.*
Consisting of a large number of objects; extreme. Used very loosely. Example: "This program produces infinite garbage." "He is an infinite LOSER." See HAIR.
The slang use of "infinite" is an abuse of its precise technical meaning in mathematics.

INTERCAL *(int':r-cal)* *noun.*
A computer language designed by Donald R. Woods and James M. Lyon. INTERCAL is purposely different from any other computer language in all ways but one: it is purely a written language, being totally unspeakable.
The name "INTERCAL" is an abbreviation for "Compiler

Language With No Pronounceable Acronym."

An excerpt from the INTERCAL Reference Manual will make the style of the language clear. In most programming languages, if you want a variable (say A) to have the value 65536, you would write something like

LET A = 65536

or

A := 65536;

The INTERCAL Reference Manual, however, explains that "it is a well-known and oft-demonstrated fact that a person whose work is incomprehensible is held in high esteem. For example: if one were to state that the simplest way to store 65536 in an INTERCAL variable is

DO :1 < − #0¢#256

any sensible programmer would say that that was absurd. Since this is indeed the simplest method, the programmer would be made to look foolish in front of his boss, who would of course have happened to turn up, as bosses are wont to do. The effect would be no less devastating for the programmer having been correct."

INTERCAL has many other peculiar features, as well, to make it even more unspeakable. The language was actually implemented and used by many people at Princeton University.

See CHARACTERS for a discussion of names of characters in INTERCAL.

IRP *(urp) verb.*

To perform a series of tasks repeatedly with a minor change each time through. A hacker who is also a teaching assistant might say, "I guess I'll IRP over these homework papers and give each a RANDOM grade."

The word "IRP" is an acronym for "Indefinite RePeat." It is the name of a command in the MIDAS assembler, a program that translates PDP-10 instructions from a symbolic form to binary bits.

JEDGAR *(jed'g:r)*

A "counterspy" program. See OUTPUT SPY.

JFCL *(j:-fik':l, jif'k:l) verb.*

To cancel or annul something. "Why don't you jfcl that out?"

The PDP-10 has several instructions that don't do anything (remember that SKIP means "Do not SKIP," as explained in the entry for AOS). However, the fastest do-nothing instruction happens to be JFCL, which stands for "Jump if Flag set and then CLear the flag." This does something useful, but is a very fast no-operation if no flag is specified.

If one wants to patch a program by removing one instruction, the easiest thing to do is to replace the instruction with one that doesn't do anything. Such an instruction is said to have been jfcl'd out. This bit of jargon was then extended metaphorically.

The license plate on hacker Geoff Goodfellow's BMW is JFCL.

JIFFY *(jif'ee) noun.*

1. The time unit used by a clock attached to a computer to measure CPU time, typically either 1/60 second or (less commonly) one millisecond. "The swapper runs every six jiffies" means that the virtual memory management routine is executed once for every six ticks of the computer's clock, or ten times a second.

2. An indeterminate time from a few seconds to forever. "I'll do it in a jiffy" means certainly not now and possibly never. This is a bit contrary to the more widespread use of the word.

JOCK *noun.*

A programmer who is characterized by the large and somewhat brute-force programs he writes. Brute-force programs typically work by enumerating all possible combinations of things in an effort to find the one combination that solves the problem. An example of a brute-force program is one that sorts ten thousand numbers by examining them all, picking the smallest one, and saving it in another table; then examining all the numbers again and picking the smallest one except for the one it already picked; and in general choosing the next number by examining all ten thousand numbers and choosing the smallest one that hasn't yet been picked (as determined by examining all the ones already picked). Yes, the program will produce the right answer, but it will be much slower than a program that uses even a modicum of cleverness to avoid most of the work. (A little bit of computer science—specifically, the theory of algorithms—will show that a typical large computer such as a PDP-10, using a clever sorting method, can sort ten thousand numbers in about eight seconds, while the brute-force method outlined above would take about 40 days.)

J. RANDOM *(jay' ran'd:m) adjective.*
Arbitrary; ordinary; any one; "any old." "Would you let J. Random LOSER marry your daughter?" See RANDOM.

JRST *(jurst) verb.*
1. To suddenly change subjects, with no intention of returning to the previous topic. Usage: rare and considered silly.
2. To jump. "Jack be nimble, Jack be quick, Jack jrst over the candle stick." This is even sillier.
  The PDP-10 JUMP instruction means "Do not jump," as explained in the definition of AOS. The JUMPA instruction ("JUMP Always") does jump, but it isn't quite so fast as the JRST instruction ("Jump and ReSTore flags"). The instruction is used so frequently that the speed matters, so all PDP-10 hackers automatically use the faster though more obscure JRST instruction.

KLUGE, KLUDGE *(klooj) noun.*
1. A Rube Goldberg device in hardware or software.
2. A clever programming trick intended to solve a particularly nasty case in an efficient, if not clear, manner. Often used to repair BUGS. Often verges on being a CROCK.
3. Something that works for the wrong reason.
4. *verb.* To insert a kluge into a program. "I've kluged this routine to get around that weird bug, but there's probably a better way." Also "kluge up."
5. A feature that is implemented in a RUDE manner.
  KLUGE AROUND. To avoid (a problem) by inserting a kluge.

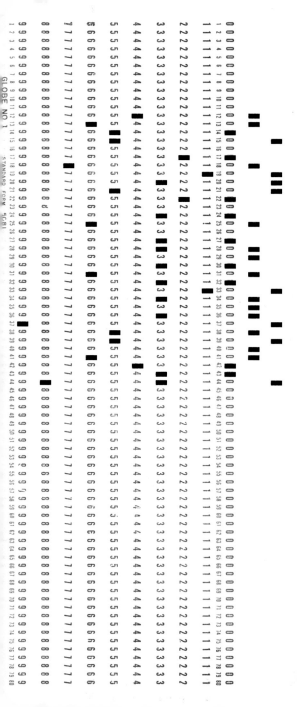

Steve,
Parse:

SAGA
PHASE OF THE MOON
PARSE
MAGIC (2)
EL CAMINO BIGNUM
LOGICAL
J. RANDOM

Is ATLAS Telecom crufty
or cuspy?

LASER CHICKEN *noun.*
Kung Pao Chicken, a standard Chinese dish containing chicken, peanuts, and bell peppers in a spicy pepper-oil sauce. A few hackers call it "laser chicken" for two reasons: It can ZAP you just like a laser, and the pepper-oil sauce has a red color reminiscent of a laser beam.

LIFE *noun.*
A cellular-automaton game invented by mathematician John Horton Conway, and first introduced publicly by Martin Gardner in his column "Mathematical Games" (*Scientific American,* October 1970). Hackers at various places contributed to the mathematical analysis of this game, notably Bill Gosper at MIT. When a hacker mentions "life," he is much more likely to mean this game than the magazine, the breakfast cereal, or the human state of existence.

LINE FEED
1. *verb.* To feed the paper through a terminal by one line (in order to print on the next line). On a display terminal, to move the cursor down to the next line of the screen.
2. *noun.* The "character" which, when sent to a terminal by the computer, causes the terminal to perform this action.
   This is standard ASCII terminology.

LINE STARVE
1. *verb.* To feed the paper through the terminal the wrong way by one line. (Most terminals can't do this!) On a display terminal, to move the cursor up to the previous line of the screen. Example: "To print X squared, you just output X, line starve, 2, line feed." (The line starve causes the "2" to appear on the line above the "X," and the line feed gets back to the original line.)
2. *noun.* A "character" (or character sequence) that causes a terminal to perform this action.
   This is *not* standard ASCII terminology. Even among hackers it is considered a bit silly.

LOGICAL *adjective.*
Conventional; assumed for the sake of exposition or convenience; not the actual thing but in some sense equivalent to it;

not necessarily corresponding to reality. Example: If a person who had long held a certain post (for example, Les Earnest at Stanford) left and was replaced, the replacement would for a while be known as the "logical Les Earnest." Pepsi might be referred to as "logical Coke" (or vice versa).

At Stanford, "logical" compass directions denote a coordinate system in which "logical north" is toward San Francisco, "logical south" is toward San Jose, "logical west" is toward the ocean, and "logical east" is away from the ocean—even though logical north varies between physical (true) north near San Francisco and physical west near San Jose. The best rule of thumb here is that El Camino Real by definition always runs logical north-and-south. In giving directions, one might say, "To get to Rincon Tarasco Restaurant, get onto EL CAMINO BIGNUM going logical north." Using the word "logical" helps to prevent the recipient from worrying about the fact that the sun is setting almost directly in front of him as he travels "north."

A similar situation exists at MIT. Route 128 (famous for the electronics industries that have grown up along it) is a three-quarters circle surrounding Boston at a radius of ten miles, terminating at the coast line at each end. It would be most precise to describe the two directions along this highway as being "clockwise" and "counterclockwise," but the road signs all say "north" and "south," respectively. A hacker would describe these directions as "logical north" and "logical south," to indicate that they are conventional directions not corresponding to the usual convention for those words. (If you went logical south along the entire length of Route 128, you would start out going northwest, curve around to the south, and finish headed due east!)

Synonym: VIRTUAL. Antonym: physical.

This use is an extension from its technical use in computer science. A program can be written to do input or output using a "logical device." When the program is run, the user can specify which "physical" (actual) device to use for that logical device. For example, a program might send all its error messages to a logical device called ERROR; the user can then specify whether logical device ERROR should be the terminal, a disk file, or the NULL DEVICE (to throw the error messages away).

A speculation is that the word "logical" is used because, even though a thing isn't the actual object in question, you can reason logically about the thing as if it were the actual object.

LOSE *verb.*
1. To fail. A program loses when it encounters an exceptional condition or fails to work in the expected manner.
2. To be exceptionally unaesthetic.
3. Of people, to be obnoxious or unusually stupid (as opposed to ignorant). See LOSER.

DESERVE TO LOSE *verb.* Said of someone who willfully does THE WRONG THING, or uses a feature known to be MARGINAL. What is meant is that one deserves the consequences of one's losing actions. "Boy, anyone who tries to use UNIX deserves to lose!"

LOSE, LOSE *interjection.* A reply or comment on an undesirable situation. Example: "I accidentally deleted all my files!" "Lose, lose."

LOSER *noun.* An unexpectedly bad situation, program, programmer, or person. Someone who habitually loses (even winners can lose occasionally). Someone who knows not and knows not that he knows not.

Emphatic forms are "real loser," "total loser," and "complete loser" (but not "MOBY loser," which would be a contradiction in terms).

LOSS *noun.* Something (but not a person) that loses: a situation in which something is losing. Emphatic forms are "MOBY loss," "total loss," "complete loss." (Note that a *loss* can be moby even though a *loser* cannot be.)

WHAT A LOSS! *interjection.* A remark to the effect that a situation is bad. Example: Suppose someone said, "Fred decided to write his program in ADA instead of LISP." The reply "What a loss!" comments that the choice was bad, or that it will result in an undesirable situation—but may also implicitly recognize that Fred was forced to make that decision because of outside influences. On the other hand, the reply "What a loser!" is a more general remark about Fred himself, and implies that bad consequences will be entirely his fault.

LOSSAGE *(lawss':j) noun.* The stuff of which losses are made. This is a collective noun. "What a loss!" and "What lossage!" are nearly synonymous remarks.

LPT *(lip':t) noun.*
A Line PrinTer. "The LIST command can be used to send a file to the lpt."

LUSER *(loo'z:r) noun.*
A USER who is probably also a LOSER. ("Luser" and "loser" are pronounced identically.)

This word was coined about eight years ago at MIT. When you first walk up to a terminal at MIT and type "Control-Z" to get the computer's attention, it prints out some status information, including how many people are already using the computer. It might print "14 users," for example. Someone thought it would be a great joke to patch the SYSTEM to print "14 losers" instead. There ensued a great controversy, as some of the users didn't particularly want to be called losers to their faces every time they used the computer. For a while several hackers struggled covertly, each changing the message behind the back of the others; any time you logged into the computer it was even money whether it would say "users" or "losers." Finally, someone tried the compromise "lusers," and it stuck. To this day, when you connect to the MIT computer, it will say "14 lusers."

MACROTAPE *(mak'roh-tayp) noun.*
An industry standard reel of magnetic tape, about ten inches in diameter, as opposed to a MICROTAPE.

MAGIC *adjective.*
1. As yet unexplained, or too complicated to explain. (Arthur C. Clarke once said that any sufficiently advanced technology is indistinguishable from magic.) "The precise form in which CHARACTERS are printed to the terminal is controlled

by a number of magic BITS." "This routine magically com-
putes the parity of an eight-bit byte in only three instructions."
2. Characteristic of something that works though no one really
understands why.
3. Characteristic of a FEATURE not generally publicized which
allows something otherwise impossible—or a feature for-
merly in that category but now unveiled. Example: the keyboard commands at Stanford that override the screen-hid-
ing features.
   See AUTOMAGICALLY.

(1) When Barbara Steele was pregnant, her doctor had her take
a sonogram to determine whether she was carrying twins.
Now, Barbara and I had both studied computer science at MIT,
and we saw that some complex computerized image-process-
ing was involved. We asked the doctor how it was done, hoping
to learn some details about the mathematics involved in the
computer program. The doctor simply said, "The probe sends
out sound waves, which bounce off the internal organs. A mi-
crophone picks up the echoes, like radar, and sends the signals
to a computer—and the computer makes a picture." Thanks a
lot! Now a hacker would have said, ". . . and the computer
magically makes a picture," implicitly acknowledging that he
had glossed over an extremely complicated process.

(2) Some years ago I was snooping around in the cabinets that
housed the MIT AI lab's PDP-10, and I noticed a little switch
glued to the frame of one cabinet. It was obviously a home-
brew job added by one of the lab's hardware hackers (no one
knows who).
   You don't touch an unknown switch on a computer without
knowing what it does, because you might CRASH it. The switch
was labeled in a most unhelpful way. It had two positions, and
scrawled in pencil on the metal switch body were the words
"magic" and "more magic." The switch was in the "more
magic" position.
   I called another hacker over to look at it. He had never seen
the switch before, either. Closer examination revealed that the

switch only had one wire running to it! The other end of the wire did disappear into the maze of wires inside the computer, but it's a basic fact of electricity that a switch can't do anything unless there are two wires connected to it. This switch had a wire connected on one side and no wire on its other side.

It was clear that this switch was someone's idea of a silly joke. Convinced by our reasoning that the switch was inoperative, we flipped it. The computer instantly crashed!

Imagine our utter astonishment. We wrote it off as coincidence, but nevertheless restored the switch to the "more magic" position before reviving the computer.

A year later, I told this story to yet another hacker—David Moon, as I recall. (See MOON.) He clearly doubted my sanity, or suspected me of a supernatural belief in the power of this switch, or perhaps thought I was fooling him with a BOGUS SAGA. To prove it to him, I showed him the very switch, still glued to the cabinet frame with only one wire connected to it. It was still in the "more magic" position. We scrutinized the switch and its lone connection and found that the other end of the wire, though connected to the computer wiring, was connected to a ground pin. That clearly made the switch doubly useless: not only was it electrically nonoperative, but it was connected to a place that couldn't affect anything anyway. So we flipped the switch.

The computer promptly crashed.

This time we ran for Richard Greenblatt, a long-time MIT hacker who was close at hand. He had never noticed the switch before, either. He inspected it, concluded it was useless, got some diagonal cutters and DIKED IT OUT. We then revived the computer, and it has run fine ever since.

We still don't know how the switch crashed the machine. There is a theory that some circuit near the ground pin was MARGINAL, and flipping the switch changed the electrical capacitance enough to upset the circuit as millionth-of-a-second pulses went through it. But we'll never know for sure. All we can really say is that the switch was magic.

I still have that switch in my basement. Maybe I'm silly, but I usually keep it set on "more magic."

MARGINAL *adjective.*
1. Extremely small. "A marginal increase in memory can decrease GC time drastically." (In everyday terms, this means that it's a lot easier to clean off your desk if you have a spare place to put some of the junk while you sort through it.) See EPSILON.
2. Of extremely small merit. "This proposed new FEATURE seems rather marginal to me."
3. Of extremely small probability of WINNING; on the edge of LOSING. "The power supply was rather marginal anyway; no wonder it FRIED."

    MARGINALLY *adverb.* Slightly; somewhat. "The RAVS (raviolis) here are only marginally better than at Small Eating Place."

    MARGINAL HACKS *noun.* Margaret Jacks Hall, a building into which the Stanford Computer Science Department was recently moved.

MESH *noun.*
The character "#" (number sign).
    Synonyms: CRUNCH, SPLAT. See CHARACTERS.

MICROTAPE *(miek'roh-tayp) noun.*
A DECtape, as opposed to a MACROTAPE. A DECtape is a small reel of magnetic tape about four inches in diameter and an inch wide. Unlike standard magnetic tapes, microtapes allow "random access" to the data. In their heyday they were used in pretty much the same ways one would now use a floppy disk: as a small, portable way to save and transport files and programs. Apparently the term "microtape" was actually the official term used within DEC for these tapes until someone CONSED UP the word "DECtape," which of course has more commercial appeal.

MISFEATURE *noun.*
A FEATURE that eventually clobbers someone, possibly because it is not adequate for a new situation that has evolved. It is not the same as a BUG because fixing it involves a gross philosophical change to the system's structure. A misfeature is different

from a simple and unforeseen side effect. The term implies that the misfeature was carefully planned, but that not all the consequences or circumstances were predicted accurately. This is different from just not having thought ahead at all. Often a feature becomes a misfeature because a trade-off is made.

Example: "Well, yeah, it's kind of a misfeature that file names are limited to six characters. That decision was made N years ago to simplify the file access software and save space on the disk, and now we're stuck with it."

MOBY *(moh'bee)*

1. *adjective.* Large, immense, complex, impressive. Examples: "A Saturn V rocket is a truly moby FROB." (This example is oxymoronic—frobs are normally not very large.) "Some MIT undergrads pulled off a moby HACK at the Harvard–Yale game."

2. *noun.* The total size of a computer's address space, that is, the amount of memory that a given computer can access. Examples: For a PDP-10, a moby is 262144 36-bit words; for a PDP-8, it is 4096 12-bit words; for a 68000 or a VAX, it is 4294967296 8-bit bytes. This term is useful because when a computer has "virtual memory mapping," a computer may have more physical memory attached to it than any one program can access directly. One can then say, "This computer has six mobies" to mean that the ratio of physical memory to address space is six—without having to say specifically how much memory there actually is. That in turn implies that the computer can time-share six "full-sized" programs without having to swap programs between memory and disk. If a computer has exactly two mobies, then the one with smaller (physical) addresses is called the "low moby" and the other one is called the "high moby." Example: "Response times will be long today. The high moby just FRIED, so we're limping along with only half our memory."

3. *noun.* 256K 36-bit words, which is the size of a moby on every hacker's favorite computer, the PDP-10. This amount is sufficiently close to a megabyte (one million bytes) that

sometimes the terms "moby" and "megabyte" are used interchangeably.

4. *adjective.* An honorific term of address (never of third-person reference) usually used to show admiration, respect, and/or friendliness to a competent hacker. Example: "So, moby Knight, how's the CONS machine doing?" (Tom Knight was one of the designers of MIT's LISP Machine, a personal computer designed to run LISP. The prototype was called "CONS.")

5. *adjective.* In backgammon, doubles on the dice, as in "moby sixes," "moby threes," "moby ones," etc. Compare this with BIGNUMS: Double sixes are both bignums and moby sixes, but moby ones are not bignums. (The use of term "moby" to describe double ones is sarcastic.)

MOBY FOO, MOBY LOSS, MOBY HACK, MOBY WIN. These are standard emphatic forms.

MODE *noun.*
A general state, usually used with an adjective or noun describing the state. Use of the word "mode" rather than "STATE" implies that the state is extended over time, and probably also that some activity characteristic of that state is being carried out. Examples: "No time to HACK; I'm in thesis mode." "I'll be in vacation mode next week." "My editor is stuck in some weird mode where every CHARACTER I type appears twice on the screen." "The E editor normally uses a display terminal, but if you're on a TTY it will switch to nondisplay mode."

This term is normally used in a technical sense to describe the state of a program. Extended usage—for example, to describe people—is definitely slang.

See DAY MODE, NIGHT MODE, and YOYO MODE; also COM MODE, TALK MODE, and GABRIEL MODE.

MODULO *(mahd'yoo-loh) preposition.*
Except for. This is from mathematical terminology. One writes "4≡22 mod 9" to mean that 4 and 22 give the same remainder when divided by 9 (the precise meaning is a bit more complicated, but that's the idea). One might say that that 4 equals 22 "except for some 9's," because if you add two 9's to 4 you get

22. Examples: "Well, LISP seems to work okay now, modulo that GC BUG." "I feel fine today modulo a slight headache."

MOON *noun.*
1. A celestial object whose phase is very important to hackers. See PHASE OF THE MOON.
2. The login name of MIT hacker David A. Moon. Because he hacks important system software, his PHASE may also be very important to hackers.

MUMBLAGE *(muhm'bl:j) noun.*
The topic of one's mumbling. (See MUMBLE.) "All that mumblage" is used like "all that stuff" when it is not quite clear what it is or how it works, or like "all that crap" when "mumble" is being used as an implicit replacement for obscenities.

MUMBLE *interjection.*
1. Said when the correct response is too complicated to enunciate or the speaker has not thought it out. Often prefaces a longer answer, or indicates a general reluctance to get into a big long discussion. Example: "Don't you think that we could improve LISP performance by using a hybrid reference-count transaction garbage collector, if the cache is big enough and there are some extra cache BITS for the microcode to use?" "Well, mumble . . . I'll have to think about it."
2. Sometimes used as an expression of disagreement. "I think we should buy a VAX." "Mumble!" Common variant: Mumble frotz. (See FROTZ.)
3. Yet another metasyntactic variable like FOO.

MUNCH *verb.*
To transform information in a serial fashion, often requiring large amounts of computation. To trace down a data structure.
Synonyms: CRUNCH, GROVEL. "Munch" connotes somewhat less pain than the other two words.

MUNCHING SQUARES *noun.*
A display HACK dating back to the PDP-1 (early 1960s) at MIT, which employs a trivial computation (involving XOR'ing of x–y

display coordinates, described in items 146–148 of HAKMEM) to produce an impressive display of moving, growing, and shrinking squares. The hack usually has a parameter (usually taken from toggle switches) which, when well chosen, can produce amazing effects. Some of these, discovered recently on the LISP machine, have been christened "munching triangles," "munching w's," and "munching mazes." More generally, suppose a graphics program produces an impressive and ever-changing display of some basic form FOO on a display terminal, and does it using a relatively simple program; then the program (or the resulting display) is likely to be referred to as "munching foos." [By the way, note the use of the word *foo* as a metasyntactic variable in the last sentence.]

MUNG *(muhng) verb.*
1. To make changes to a file, often large-scale, usually irrevocable, occasionally accidental.
2. To destroy, usually accidentally, occasionally maliciously. Note that the SYSTEM only mungs things maliciously (this is a consequence of Murphy's Law).
3. The kind of beans of which the sprouts are used in Chinese food. (That's their real name! Mung beans! Really!)
    This word is said to be a recursive acronym: MUNG means Mung Until No Good.
    MUNGE *(muhnj) verb.*   Variant of MUNG.

N *(en) noun.*
1. Some large and indeterminate number. "There were N bugs in that crock!"
2. An arbitrarily large (and perhaps infinite) number.
3. A variable whose value is specified by the current context. For example: When ordering a meal at a restaurant, "N" may refer to however many people there are at the table. From the remark "We'd like to order N wonton soups and a family dinner for N minus one," you can deduce that one person at the table wants to eat only soup, even though you don't know how many people there are. A silly riddle: "How many computers does it take to shift the bits in a register?" "$N+1$: N to hold all the bits still, and one to shove the register over."

NTH *(enth) adjective.* The ordinal counterpart of N. "Now, for the Nth and last time . . ." In the specific context "Nth-year graduate student," N is generally assumed to be at least 4, and is usually 5 or more.

See also 69.

NIGHT MODE *noun.*

The state a person is in when he is working at night and sleeping during the day. (The advantage of being in night mode is that the computers are usually overloaded during the day; at night more CYCLES are available.)

See PHASE and DAY MODE.

NIL *(nil)*

No. This word is used in reply to a question, particularly one asked using the "-P" convention. Example: "Foodp?" "Nil." That simple interchange means "Do you want to come eat with us?" "No, thanks." See T. (In the LISP language, the name "nil" means "false," among other things.)

NULL DEVICE *noun.*

An input/output device that doesn't do anything. A card reader reads cards, and a terminal keyboard reads the characters typed on the keyboard, but reading from the null device always yields zeros. Similarly, writing to a printer produces words on paper, but writing to the null device just throws the output into the BIT BUCKET.

There is no such physical thing as a null device—it would be pointless to build one—but it is a useful notion that is provided LOGICALLY by many operating systems. If a program normally prints out a lot of information and you don't happen to want to see it, you simply direct the program to send the output to the null device. The program is satisfied because it has a device to print on, and you're happy because the output is AUTOMAGI-CALLY discarded without wasting paper.

NXM *(niks':m)*

A lapse of memory; a GLITCH. This phrase is an acronym for "NoneXistent Memory," the result of accessing a computer's memory at an address for which no memory has been connected. A NXM is technically a special case of an ILL MEM REF, but in slang usage they are practically synonymous.

OBSCURE *adjective.*

Little-known; incomprehensible; undocumented. This word is used, in an exaggeration of its normal meaning, to imply a total lack of comprehensibility. "The reason for that last CRASH is obscure." "That program has a very obscure command syntax." "This KLUDGE works by taking advantage of an obscure FEATURE in TECO." The phrase "moderately obscure" implies that it could be figured out but probably isn't worth the trouble.

OPEN *noun.*

A left parenthesis, "(". This word is used as shorthand to eliminate ambiguity when communicating a sequence of characters vocally. To read aloud the LISP program "(DEFUN FOO (X) (PLUS X 1))," which takes an argument X and adds 1 to it, one might say: "Open def-fun foo. Open eks close. Open, plus eks one, close, close." See CLOSE.

> **OPEN BRACKET** *noun.*   The character "[".
> **OPEN BRACE** *noun.*   The character "{".

OUTPUT SPY *noun.*

On the MIT system there is a program that allows you to see what is being printed on someone else's terminal. It works by "spying" on the other guy's output, by examining the insides of the monitor system. It can do this because the MIT system purposely has very little in the way of "protection" that prevents one user from interfering with another. Fair is fair, however. There is another program that will automatically notify you if anyone starts to spy on your output. It works in exactly the same way, by looking at the insides of the operating system to see if anyone else is looking at the insides that have to do with your output. This "counterspy" program is called JEDGAR (pronounced as two syllables: jed'gar), in honor of the former head of the FBI.

By the way, the output spy program is called "os" *(oh'ess')*. Throughout the rest of computer science, and also at IBM, "OS" means "operating system," but among MIT hackers it almost always means "output spy."

PARSE *verb.*

1. To determine the syntactic structure of a sentence or other utterance. (This is close to the standard English meaning.) Example: "That was the one I saw you." "I can't parse that."
2. More generally, to understand or comprehend. "It's very simple. You just kretch the glims and then AOS the zotz." "I can't parse that."
3. Of fish, to have to remove the bones yourself (usually at a Chinese restaurant). "I object to parsing fish" means "I don't want to get a whole fish, but a sliced one is okay." A "parsed fish" has been de-boned. There is some controversy whether "unparsed" should mean "bony," or also mean "deboned."

   This term is derived from the technical use of the word in linguistics. Hackers know about it because some researchers in artificial intelligence work on the problem of writing computer programs that can understand and/or speak human languages.

PATCH

1. *noun.* A temporary addition to a piece of code, usually as a quick-and-dirty remedy to an existing BUG or MISFEATURE. A patch may or may not work, and may or may not eventually be incorporated permanently into the program.
2. *verb.* To fix something temporarily; to insert a patch into a piece of code. See KLUGE AROUND.

PDL *(pid':l, pud':l)* [acronym for Push Down List] *noun.*

1. A last-in/first-out (LIFO) queue, also known as a "stack" in computer science; more loosely, any ordered list of things. Even more loosely, any set of things. A person's "pdl" is the set of things he has to do in the future. One speaks of the next project to be attacked as having "risen to the top of the pdl" (or the top of the stack). Examples: "I'm afraid I've got real work to do, so this HACK will have to be pushed way down on my pdl." "I haven't done it yet because every time I POP my pdl something new gets

PUSHED." If you are interrupted several times in the middle of a conversation, "my pdl overflowed" means "I forget what we were talking about originally." (The implication is that too many items were pushed onto the pdl than could be remembered, and so the least recent items were lost.) See PUSH and POP.

OVERFLOW PDL *noun.* The place where you put things when your pdl is full. If you don't have one and too many things get pushed, you forget something. The overflow pdl for a person's memory might be a memo pad.

> Hey, diddle, diddle
> The overflow pdl
>   To get a little more stack;
> If that's not enough
> Then you lose it all,
>   And have to pop all the way back.

–The Great QUUX

The term "pdl" is an acronym for Push Down List, and in its technical sense rather than its slang meaning always means a stack. The best example of a stack is to be found in a cafeteria: a pile of plates sitting on a spring in a well in a cart, so that when you put a plate on the top they all sink down; and when you take one off the top the rest spring up a bit.

PESSIMAL *adjective.*
Maximally bad. "This is a pessimal situation."

PESSIMIZE *verb.* To make as bad as possible.

PESSIMIZING COMPILER *noun.* A compiler that produces object code that is *worse* than the straightforward or obvious translation. (The implication is that the compiler is actually trying to optimize the program, but through stupidity is doing the opposite. A few pessimizing compilers have been written on purpose, however, as pranks.)

These words are the obvious Latin-based antonyms for "optimal" and "optimize," but for some reason they do not appear in most English dictionaries—although "pessimize" is listed in the Oxford English Dictionary.

PHANTOM *noun.*
At Stanford, the term "phantom" is used to mean a DRAGON.

PHASE *noun.*
The offset of one's waking-sleeping schedule with respect to the standard 24-hour cycle. This is a useful concept among people who often work at night according to no fixed schedule. Examples: "What's your phase?" "I've been getting in about eight P.M. lately, but I'm going to phase around to the day schedule by Friday." A person who is roughly 12 hours out of phase is sometimes said to be in NIGHT MODE. (The term DAY MODE is also, but less frequently, used, meaning you're working 9 to 5—or, more likely, 10 to 6.)

It is not uncommon to change one's phase by as much as six hours per day on a regular basis. For example, one can stay awake for twenty hours and then sleep for ten. This can be a bit of a strain on the metabolism when done for extended periods, however. One nice phase-changing schedule is to keep a 28-hour day: stay awake 18 hours and sleep for ten, for example. Six 28-hour days are equal to seven 24-hour days, so this schedule means you can be in day mode on weekends and in night mode (or close to it) for most weekdays; that way you get lots of CYCLES by being awake at night and yet are reasonably synchronized with the REAL WORLD on weekends.

CHANGE PHASE THE HARD WAY. To stay awake for a very long time in order to get into a different phase.

CHANGE PHASE THE EASY WAY. To stay asleep for a very long time in order to get into a different phase.

The phenomenon of "jet lag" that afflicts travelers who cross many time-zone boundaries may be attributed to two distinct causes: the strain of travel per se, and the strain of changing phase. Hackers who suddenly find that they must change phase drastically in a short period of time, particularly the hard way, experience something very like jet lag without traveling.

PHASE OF THE MOON *noun.*
A random parameter on which something is (humorously) said to depend. Something that depends on the phase of the moon

is at best unpredictable, at worst unreliable. (Maybe it is predictable, but figuring it out is so complicated it isn't worth it.) Example: "Whether the editor will save your file automatically when you exit depends on the phase of the moon."

The "phase of the moon" is one example of RANDOMNESS.

Once a program written by Gerald Sussman (professor of electrical engineering at MIT) and Guy Steele had a BUG that really did depend on the phase of the moon! There is a little subroutine that has traditionally been used in various programs at MIT to calculate an approximation to the moon's true phase; the phase is then printed out—at the top of program listings, for example—along with the date and time, purely for fun. (Actually, since hackers spend most of their time indoors, this might be the only way they would ever know what the moon's phase was!) Steele incorporated this routine into a LISP program that, when it wrote out a file, would print a 'timestamp" at the top that looked something like this:

```
;THE MOON IS 1 DAY, 20 HOURS, 42 MINUTES, AND 54 SECONDS
;   PAST THE FIRST QUARTER.
;THE SUN IS 41*44'1" NORTH OF EAST,
;   35*7'26" BELOW THE HORIZON.
;THAT MEANS IT IS NOW 2:21 A.M.
;   ON WEDNESDAY, MARCH 23, 1983.
```

(A calculation of the position of the sun was also included for additional HACK VALUE. The asterisk was used in lieu of a "degrees" symbol to indicate angles.) Occasionally the first line of the message would be too long and would overflow onto the next line like this:

```
;THE MOON IS 2 DAYS, 17 HOURS, 20 MINUTES, AND 45 SECONDS
;   PAST THE FIRST QUARTER.
;THE SUN IS 18*17'47" WEST OF NORTH,
;   44*56'42" BELOW THE HORIZON.
;THAT MEANS IT IS NOW 10:59 P.M.
;   ON WEDNESDAY, MARCH 23, 1983.
```

When the file was later read back in, the program would BARF. The length of the first line depended on the precise time when the timestamp was printed, and so the bug literally depended on the phase of the moon!

POM *(pee-oh-em, pahm) noun.* An abbreviation for PHASE OF THE MOON. This is usually used in the phrase "POM-dependent," meaning FLAKEY.

POP *verb.*

1. To remove something from a stack or PDL. If a person says he has popped something from his pdl, he means he has finally finished working on it and can now remove it from the list of things hanging over his head.
2. To return from a digression. The term "popj" *(pop'jay)* is also used in this sense. "Popj?" as a simple request means "Have we finished with this digression? Shall we return to the previous subject of conversation?" "Popj!" has more the force of "Stop FLAMING about that, you LOSER! Let's return to the main point." "Popj, popj" means roughly "Now let's see, where were we?"

   Synonym: CONTROL-P.

   Antonyms: PUSH, PUSHJ.

   The PDP-10 has instructions named POP and POPJ; the former pops a single word from a stack, and the latter (POP and Jump always) is a subroutine return instruction.

PPN *(pip':n)*

1. A combination of a "project identifier" and "programmer name," used to identify a specific file directory belonging to that programmer. This is used in the TOPS-10 operating system that DEC provides for the PDP-10. The implicit assumption is that there will be many projects, each with several programmers working on it, and that a programmer may work on several projects. This is not a bad organization; what is totally BOGUS is that projects and programmers are identified by octal (base eight) numbers! Hence the term Project-Programmer Number, or PPN. If I were programmer 72534 and wanted to work on project 306, I would have to tell the computer "login 306,72534." This is totally ridiculous. At CMU the TOPS-10 system was modified to be somewhat less ridiculous. Projects are identified by a letter and three deci-

mal (not octal) digits, and a programmer is identified by his two initials, a digit indicating the first year he came to CMU, and a fourth character that is used to distinguish between, say, Fred Loser and Farley Luser who both happened to arrive the same year. So to use the PDP-10 at CMU one might say "login A780GS70." The programmer name "GS70" is also called a "man number" at CMU, even though it isn't really a number. At Stanford, projects and programmers are identified by three letters or digits each. To work on a LISP project at Stanford, I might log in as "login lsp,gls." This is much more mnemonic. Programmer identifiers at Stanford are usually the programmer's initials, though sometimes they are nicknames or other three-letter sequences. Even though the CMU and Stanford forms are not really (pairs of) numbers, the term "ppn" is used to refer to the combination.

2. At Stanford, the term "ppn" is often used loosely to refer to the programmer name alone. "I want to send you some mail. What's your ppn?"

MIT uses an operating system called ITS that is completely unrelated to TOPS-10. ITS does not use ppn's. The closest approximation to a ppn on ITS is UNAME (user name), which is a six-character programmer name with no project number.

The names JRN and JRL are sometimes used as example names when discussing ppn's; they are understood to be programmer names for (fictitious) programmers named "J. Random Nerd" and "J. Random Loser." (See J. RANDOM.) For example, one might say "To log in, type log one comma jay are en" (that is, "log 1, JRN"). And the listener will understand that he should use his own programmer name in place of "JRN."

PROTOCOL
See DO PROTOCOL.

PSEUDOPRIME *(soo'doh-priem) noun.*
A backgammon prime (six consecutive occupied points) with one point missing; that is, only five out of six consecutive points are really occupied.

This term is a pun. In mathematics, a pseudoprime is an integer that satisfies one of a set of criteria. Any number that passes even one of these tests is almost certainly a true prime (an interger that cannot be divided evenly by any integer except itself or 1); however, there are a very few integers that can fool the tests, so the best you can say is that a number that passes the test is "probably" prime. The hacker backgammon usage stems from the idea that a pseudoprime is almost as good as a prime: it does the job of a prime for most purposes until proven otherwise, and that probably won't happen. A true backgammon prime guarantees that your opponent cannot escape; a backgammon pseudoprime will probably prevent the opponent from escaping.

PUNT *verb.*
To give up; to decide not to do. Typically there is no intention of trying again later. Examples: "Let's punt the movie tonight." "I was going to HACK all night to get this FEATURE in, but I decided to punt" may mean that you've decided not to stay up all night, and may also mean you're not ever even going to put in the feature.

This doubtless comes from football: When you punt, you give up the offense.

PUSH *verb.*
1. To put something onto a stack or PDL. If a person says something has been pushed onto his pdl, he means yet another thing has been added to the list of things hanging over his head for him to do.
2. To enter upon a digression; to save the current discussion for later. The term PUSHJ *(push'jay)* is also used in this sense. "Pushj?" means "May I interrupt for a moment?"
   Antonyms: POP, POPJ.
   Synonym: CONTROL-B.
   The PDP-10 has instructions named PUSH and PUSHJ; the former pushes a single word onto a stack, and the latter (PUSH and Jump always) is a subroutine call instruction.

QUADRUPLE BUCKY *adjective.*
1. Using all four of the shifting keys "control," "meta,"

"hyper," and "super" while typing a character key (on an MIT keyboard that has all these keys). This combination is very seldom used in practice, because when you invent a new command you usually assign it to some character that is easier to type than using all four shift keys. If you want to imply that a program has ridiculously many commands or features, you can say something like "Oh, the command that makes it spin all the tapes while whistling Beethoven's Fifth Symphony is quadruple bucky COKEBOTTLE."

2. Using four shift keys while typing a fifth character, where the four shift keys are the "control" and "meta" keys on *both* sides of the (MIT or Stanford) keyboard. This is very difficult to do! One accepted technique is to press the left-control and left-meta keys with your left hand, the right-control and right-meta keys with your right hand, and the fifth key with your nose. Such hard-to-type commands are used for things that you want to be very sure can't happen accidentally, such as throwing away your entire program and starting all over.

For a complete explanation, see BUCKY BITS.

QUES *(kwess)*
1. *noun.* The question mark character ("?").
2. *interjection.* What? Also Ques, Ques? See WALL.

QUUX *(kwuhks)*
Originally, a meta-word like FOO. This word was coined by Guy Steele for precisely this purpose when he was young and naive and not yet interacting with the real hacker community. Had he known that "foo" was the standard, he would not have bothered. Many people invent such silly words; this one seems simply to have been lucky enough to have spread a little. In an eloquent display of poetic justice, it has returned to the originator in the form of a nickname as punishment for inventing this BLETCHEROUS word in the first place.

QUUXY *(kwuhks'ee) adjective.* Of or pertaining to a QUUX.

RANDOM
1. *adjective.* Unpredictable (closest to mathematical defini-

tion); weird. "The SYSTEM's been behaving pretty randomly."
2. Assorted; various; undistinguished; uninteresting. "Who was at the conference?" "Just a bunch of random business types."
3. Frivolous; unproductive; undirected. "He's just a random LOSER."
4. Incoherent or inelegant; not well organized. "The program has a random set of MISFEATURES." "That's a random name for that function." "Well, all the names were chosen pretty randomly."
5. Gratuitously wrong; poorly done and for no good apparent reason. "This subroutine randomly uses six registers where two would have sufficed."
6. In no particular order, though deterministic. "The I/O channels are in a pool, and when a file is opened one is chosen randomly."
7. *noun.* A random hacker. This is used particularly of high school students who soak up computer time and generally get in the way. The term "high school random" is frequently heard.
8. One who lives at Random Hall at MIT.

    J. RANDOM is often prefixed to a noun to make a "name" out of it (by analogy to common names such as "J. Fred Muggs"). It means roughly "some particular" or "any specific one." The most common uses are "J. Random Loser" and "J. Random Nerd." Example: "Should J. Random Loser be allowed to delete system files without warning?"

RANDOMNESS *noun.*
1. An unexplainable MISFEATURE; gratuitous inelegance or inconsistency; failure to do THE RIGHT THING.
2. A HACK or CROCK that depends on a complex combination of coincidences; also, the combination upon which the hack or crock depends for its accidental failure to malfunction; a situation in which several BUGS or MISFEATURES happen to cancel each other.
    See also PHASE OF THE MOON.

RAPE *verb.*

To (metaphorically) screw someone or something, violently; in particular, to destroy a program or information irrecoverably. This term is usually used in describing damage to the file system (that portion of the computer system responsible for keeping track of all files and maintaining their integrity). Example: "Some LOSER ran a program that did direct output to the disk instead of going through the file system and ended up raping the master file directory."

RAV *(rav) noun.*

A Chinese appetizer known variously in the plural as Peking ravioli, dumplings, and potstickers. The term "rav" is short for "ravioli," which among hackers always means the Chinese kind rather than the Italian kind. Both consist of a filling in a pasta shell, but the Chinese kind uses a thinner pasta and is cooked differently, either by steaming or frying. A rav or dumpling can be steamed or fried, but a potsticker is always the fried kind (so called because it sticks to the frying pot and has to be scraped off). "Let's get hot-and-sour soup and three orders of ravs."

RAVE *verb.*

1. To persist in discussing a specific subject.
2. To speak authoritatively on a subject about which one knows very little.
3. To complain (loud and long) to a person who is not in a position to correct the difficulty.
4. To purposely annoy another person verbally.
5. To proselytize (in a loose or metaphorical sense).
   Synonym: FLAME.
   This term was imported from WPI. It differs slightly from "flame" in that "rave" implies that it is the manner or persistence of speaking that is annoying, while "flame" implies somewhat more strongly that the subject matter is annoying as well.

REAL USER *noun.*

1. A commercial user; one who is paying "real" money for his computer usage.

2. A nonhacker; someone using the system for an explicit purpose (such as a research project, or academic course-work). See USER.

It is possible for one person to play different roles at different times. This is especially true of hackers who are also students. "I need this fixed so I can do a problem set. I'm not complaining out of RANDOMNESS, but as a real user."

REAL WORLD, THE *noun.*

1. Those institutions at which people might use the word "programming" in the same sentence as "FORTRAN," "COBOL," "RPG," "IBM," etc.
2. Places where programs do such commercially necessary but intellectually uninspiring things as compute payroll checks and invoices.
3. To programmers (especially hackers), the location of non-programmers and activities not related to programming.
4. A universe in which the standard dress is shirt and tie, and in which a person's working hours are defined as 9 to 5.
5. The location of the status quo.
6. Anywhere outside a university. Example: "Poor fellow, he's left MIT and gone into the real world."

This term is used pejoratively by those not in residence there. In conversation, talking of someone who has entered the real world is not unlike talking about a deceased person.

RIGHT THING, THE *noun.*

That which is "obviously" the correct or appropriate thing to use, do, say, etc. Use of this term often implies that in fact reasonable people may disagree. Examples: "Never let your conscience keep you from doing the right thing!" "What's the right thing for LISP to do when computing *a* mod 0? Should it return *a*, or give a divide-by-zero error?"

RPG *(ahr'pee'jee')* *noun.*

1. Report Program Generator, an extremely RUDE, BOGUS, and BLETCHEROUS programming language.
2. Richard P. Gabriel, a hacker at Stanford. See GABRIEL.

RUDE *adjective.*
1. Badly written (said of programs).
2. Functionally poor, such as a program that is very difficult to use because of gratuitously poor (RANDOM?) design decisions. Antonym: CUSPY.

SACRED *adjective.*
Reserved for the exclusive use of something (this is a metaphorical extension of the standard meaning). Often this means that anyone may look at the sacred object, but destroying it will cause a malfunction in whatever it is sacred to. Example: The comment "Register seven is sacred to the interrupt handler" appearing in a program would be interpreted by a hacker to mean that one part of the program, the "interrupt handler," uses register 7, and if any other part of the program changes the contents of register 7 there will be dire consequences. (This information would be useful to him if he had to change a program someone else had written; it tells him that new code added to the program must avoid using register 7.)

SAGA *noun.*
A CUSPY but BOGUS RAVING story dealing with N RANDOM BROKEN people.
Here is an example of a saga:

Jon L. White (login name JONL) and I (GLS) were office mates at MIT for many years, and worked together on the LISP language. One April we both flew from Boston to California for a week on research business, to consult face to face with some people at Stanford, particularly our common friend Richard P. Gabriel (RPG; see GABRIEL).
RPG picked us up at the San Francisco airport and drove us back to Palo Alto (going LOGICAL SOUTH on Route 101, parallel to EL CAMINO BIGNUM). Palo Alto is adjacent to Stanford University, and about forty miles south of San Francisco. We ate at The Good Earth, a "health food" restaurant, very popular, the sort whose milkshakes all contain honey and protein powder. JONL ordered such a shake—The waitress claimed the flavor of the day was "lalaberry." I still have no idea what that

might be, but it became a running joke. It was the color of raspberry, and JONL said it tasted rather bitter. I ate a better tostada there than I have ever had in a Mexican restaurant.

After this we went to the local Uncle Gaylord's Old-Fashioned Ice Cream Parlor. They make ice cream fresh daily, in a variety of intriguing flavors. It's a chain, and they have a slogan: "If you don't live near an Uncle Gaylord's—MOVE!" Also, Uncle Gaylord (a real person) wages a constant battle to force big-name ice cream makers to print their ingredients on the package (such as air and plastic and other non-natural garbage). JONL and I had first discovered Uncle Gaylord's the previous August when we had flown to a computer science conference in Berkeley, California, the first time either of us had been on the West Coast. When not in the conference sessions, we spent our time wandering the length of Telegraph Avenue, which, like Harvard Square in Cambridge, Massachusetts, in summer was lined with picturesque street vendors and interesting little shops. On that street we discovered Uncle Gaylord's Berkeley store. The ice cream there was very good. During that August visit, JONL went absolutely bananas (so to speak) over one particular flavor, ginger honey.

Therefore, after eating at The Good Earth—indeed, after every lunch and dinner and before bed during our April visit —a trip to Uncle Gaylord's (the one in Palo Alto) was mandatory. We had arrived on a Wednesday, and by Thursday evening we had been there at least four times. Each time JONL would get ginger honey ice cream and proclaim to all bystanders that "Ginger was the spice that drove the Europeans mad! That's why they sought a route to the East! They used it to preserve their otherwise off-taste meat." After the third or fourth repetition, RPG and I were getting a little tired of this spiel, and we began to paraphrase him: "Wow! Ginger! The spice that makes rotten meat taste good!" "Say! Why don't we find some dog that's been run over and sat in the sun for a week and put some *ginger* on it for dinner?!" "Right! With a lalaberry shake!" And so on. This failed to faze JONL; he took it in good humor, as long as we kept returning to Uncle Gaylord's. He loves ginger honey ice cream.

Now, RPG and his wife KBT (Kathy Tracy) were putting us up (putting up with us?) in their home for our visit, so to thank them JONL and I took them out to a nice French restaurant of their choosing. I unadventurously chose the *filet mignon,* and KBT had *je ne sais quoi du jour,* but RPG and JONL had *lapin* (rabbit). (Waitress: *"Oui,* we have fresh rabbit, fresh today." RPG: "Well, JONL, I guess we won't need any *ginger!"*)

We finished the meal late, about 11:00 P.M., which is 2:00 A.M. Boston time, so JONL and I were rather droopy. But it wasn't yet midnight. Off to Uncle Gaylord's!

Now, the French restaurant was in Redwood City, north of Palo Alto. In leaving Redwood City, we somehow got onto Route 101 going north instead of south. JONL and I wouldn't have known the difference had RPG not mentioned it. We still knew very little of the local geography. I did figure out, however, that we were headed in the direction of Berkeley, and I half-jokingly suggested that we continue north and go to Uncle Gaylord's in Berkeley.

RPG said "Fine!" and we drove on for a while and talked. I was drowsy, and JONL actually dropped off to sleep for five minutes. When he awoke, RPG said, "Gee, JONL, you must have slept all the way over the bridge!"—referring to the one spanning San Francisco Bay. Just then we came to a sign that said "University Avenue." I mumbled something about working our way over to Telegraph Avenue; RPG said "Right!" and maneuvered some more. Eventually we pulled up in front of an Uncle Gaylord's.

I hadn't really been paying attention because I was so sleepy, and I didn't really understand what was happening until RPG let me in on it a few moments later, but I was just alert enough to notice that we had somehow come to the Palo Alto Uncle Gaylord's after all.

JONL noticed the resemblance to the Palo Alto store, but hadn't caught on. He said, "This isn't the Uncle Gaylord's I went to in Berkeley! It looked like a barn! But this place looks *just like* the one back in Palo Alto!"

RPG deadpanned, "Well, this is the one *I* always come to

when I'm in Berkeley. They've got two in San Francisco, too. Remember, they're a chain."

JONL accepted this bit of wisdom. And he was not totally ignorant—He knew perfectly well that University Avenue was in Berkeley, not far from Telegraph Avenue. What he didn't know was that there is a completely different University Avenue in Palo Alto.

JONL went up to the counter and asked for ginger honey. The guy at the counter asked whether JONL would like to taste it first—evidently their standard procedure with that flavor, as not too many people like it.

JONL said, "I'm sure I like it. Just give me a cone." The guy behind the counter insisted that JONL try just a taste first. "Some people think it tastes like soap." JONL insisted, "Look, I *love* ginger. I eat Chinese food. I eat raw ginger roots. I already went through this hassle with the guy back in Palo Alto. I *know* I like that flavor!"

At the words "back in Palo Alto," the guy behind the counter got a very strange look on his face, but said nothing. KBT caught his eye and winked. Through my stupor I still hadn't quite grasped what was going on and thought RPG was rolling on the floor laughing and clutching his stomach just because JONL had launched into his spiel ("makes rotten meat a dish for a prince") for the forty-third time. At this point RPG clued me in fully.

RPG, KBT, and I retreated to a table, trying to stifle our chuckles. JONL remained at the counter, talking about ice cream with the guy b.t.c., comparing Uncle Gaylord's to other ice cream shops and generally having a good old time.

At length the g.b.t.c. said, "You really like that stuff, huh?" JONL said, "Yeah, I've been eating it constantly back in Palo Alto for the past two days. In fact, I think this batch is about as good as the cones I got back in Palo Alto!"

G.b.t.c. looked him straight in the eye and said, "You're *in* Palo Alto!"

JONL turned slowly around and saw the three of us collapse in a fit of giggles. He clapped a hand to his forehead and exclaimed, "I've been HACKED!"

SEMI

1. *(sem'ee) noun.* The semicolon character ";". Example: "Commands to GRIND are prefixed by semi-semi-star" means that grind commands (whatever they are) begin with ";;*", not with 1/4 of a star (*).

2. *(sem'ee, sem'ie)* Prefix with words such as "immediately," as a qualifier meaning "sort of" or "not really." Example: "When is the system coming up?" "Semi-immediately." (That is, maybe not for an hour.)
   See CHARACTERS.

SHIFT LEFT (RIGHT) LOGICAL *verb.*

To move oneself to the left (right). To move out of the way. As an imperative, this implies "Get out of that (my) seat! You can move to that empty one to the left (right)."

This term is used technically to describe the motions of information bits in a computer register. Most computers have specific instructions with these names to perform such motions. The slang usage asks the listener to imagine that he is a BIT and to perform the appropriate motion. Other computer instructions, such as "rotate left" and EXCH, are also used in this way. The PDP-10 instruction that performs left-shifting is called LSH *(lish)*, and so that word is sometimes used too.

SHRIEK

The exclamation point character "!".

Synonyms: BANG, EXCL. See CHARACTERS.

69 *adjective.*

A moderately large quantity. Example: "Go away, I have sixty-nine things to do before I GRONK OUT."

Actually, any number less than 100 but large enough to have no obvious special properties will be recognized as a "large number." There is no denying that 69 is the local favorite. I don't know whether its origins are related to the obscene interpretation, but I do know that 69 decimal = 105 octal, and 69 hexadecimal = 105 decimal, which is a nice property.

SLOP *noun.*

1. A one-sided FUDGE FACTOR, that is, an allowance for error

but only in one of two directions. For example, if you need a piece of wire ten feet long and have to guess when you cut it, you make very sure to cut it too long—by a large amount if necessary—rather than too short by even a little bit. You can always cut off the "slop," but you can't paste it back on again. When discrete quantities are involved, slop is sometimes introduced to avoid the possibility of a FENCEPOST ERROR.

2. The ratio of the size or speed of code generated by a compiler to that of code carefully written by hand, minus one. Suppose that you have the choice to write a program in a so-called high-level language such as LISP or PASCAL, or to hand-craft it directly in machine language. (The advantage of the former is that you can write the program more easily; the advantage of the latter is that the program may be more efficient.) Then the slop, as defined by the formula given above, is the amount of inefficiency in the final program because you used a compiler instead of hand-crafting it. This number is often used as a measure of the goodness of a compiler: slop below 5% is very good, and 10% is usually acceptable for most purposes.

The second definition of "slop" is consonant with the first under the assumption that a compiler will never produce better code than a competent hacker. However, this assumption is not always valid. Recent software technology has produced compilers that sometimes produce better code than a good hacker because the hacker will get bored hand-crafting mountains of code and therefore be less TENSE than he could be. Compilers don't get bored.

SLURP *verb.*
To read a large data file entirely into the computer's main memory before beginning to work on it. (This may be contrasted with the strategy of reading a small piece at a time, processing it, and then reading the next piece.) Example: "This program slurps in a 1024-by-1024 matrix of numbers and then CRUNCHES them using an FFT (Fast Fourier Transform)."

SMART *adjective.*
1. Said of a program or other object that does THE RIGHT

THING in a wide variety of complicated circumstances. There is a difference between calling a program smart and calling it intelligent; in particular, there do not exist any intelligent programs (although some researchers in artificial intelligence are working toward that goal).

SMART TERMINAL *noun.* A terminal that has enough computing capability to perform useful work independent of the main computer.

SMOKING CLOVER *noun.*

A psychedelic color MUNCH due to Gosper (see GOSPERISM). This is a display HACK that produces a very strong optical illusion. A series of nested, wildly colored clover-leaf patterns appear on the screen and seem to expand in size indefinitely. When the program is stopped, the patterns are frozen; but because you have been watching them expand for a while, they suddenly seem to contract.

The display changes with a speed that is awesome to anyone who is familiar with the computer hardware being used. This speed is made possible by a very clever programming technique. Also, the clover-leaf pattern is the non-obvious result of another program that is startlingly simple. For both of these reasons, as well as for the illusion, smoking clover is a favorite HACK.

SMOP *(ess'em'oh'pee')* *noun.*

An acronym for "a Small Matter Of Programming." A piece of program code, not yet written, whose anticipated length is significantly greater than its intellectual complexity.

This term is used to refer to a program that could obviously be written but is not worth the trouble. It is also used ironically to imply that a difficult problem can be easily solved because a program can be written to do it. The irony is that it is very clear that writing such a program will be a great deal of work. Example: "It's easy to change a FORTRAN compiler to compile COBOL as well; it's just a small matter of programming."

SNAIL MAIL *noun.*

Mail sent via the Postal Service rather than electronically, sometimes written as one word: SnailMail. At its worst, electronic mail usually arrives within half an hour. Compare that to the typical three days for SnailMail. If you ask a hacker for his mailing address, he will usually give you his network address for electronic mail. You have to say "What's your SnailMail address?" if you want to send him a package.

SNARF *(snahrf) verb.*
1. To grab, especially a large document or file for the purpose of using it either with or without the owner's permission. Examples: "I snarfed the DDT manual from your desk last night." "This program snarfs all the file directories and searches for files named 'DELETE. ME.'"
   SNARF DOWN. To snarf, sometimes with the connotation of absorbing, processing, or understanding. "I think I'll snarf down the list of DDT commands so I'll know what's changed recently."

SOFTWARE ROT *noun.*
A hypothetical disease the existence of which has been deduced from the observation that unused programs or FEATURES will stop working after sufficient time has passed even if "nothing has changed."
Synonym: BIT DECAY.

SOFTWARILY *(sawft-war'-:l-ee) adverb.*
In a way pertaining to software. "The system is softwarily unreliable." Note: the adjective "softwary" is *not* used. See HARDWARILY.

SOS
1. *(ess'oh-ess') noun.* A LOSING text editor. Once, back in the 1960s, when a text editor was needed for the PDP-6, a hacker CRUFTED TOGETHER a quick-and-dirty "stopgap editor" to be used until a better one was written. Unfortunately, the old one was never really discarded when new ones came along. SOS is a descendant of that editor: SOS means "Son of Stopgap." (Since then other programs similar in style to SOS have been written, notably BILOS *(bye'lohss)* the Brother-in-Law Of Stopgap.)
2. *(sahss) verb.* To subtract one from a number; to decrease the

amount of something. This SOS means "Subtract One and do not Skip"; it is an antonym of AOS, named after a PDP-10 instruction.

SPACE CADET KEYBOARD *noun.*
A computer keyboard designed at MIT and used on special LISP computers. It has *seven* shifting keys: control, meta, hyper, super, shift, top, and Greek. (See BUCKY BITS.) There are six rows of keys instead of the usual four rows, and each row of keys is half again as wide as usual. It is jocularly called a "space cadet" keyboard because when sitting at it for the first time you feel like a junior space cadet at the control panel of a rocket ship: a little bit overwhelmed by all the controls.

SPAZZ *(spaz)*
1. *verb.* To behave spastically or erratically; more often, to commit a single gross error. "I'm sorry I BROKE the LISP system last night. I was trying to fix that printing bug and must've spazzed royally."
2. *noun.* One who spazzes. "Boy, what a spazz!"
3. *noun.* The result of spazzing; spasticity. Example: "He forgot to make the routine that prints numbers handle negative numbers. In particular, trying to print -32768 gets an ILL MEM REF." "Boy, what a spazz!"

SPLAT *(splat) noun.*
1. Name used in many places (DEC, IBM, and others) for the ASCII asterisk ("*") CHARACTER.
2. Name used by some people for the ASCII number-sign ("#") character.
3. Name used by some people for the extended Stanford ASCII circle-x character "⊗". (This character is also called "circle-x," "grinch," "blobby," and "FROB," among other names.)
4. Name for the semimythical extended Stanford ASCII circle-plus character "⊕".
5. The CANONICAL name for an output routine that outputs whatever the local interpretation of "splat" is.
   Nobody really agrees what character "splat" is, but the term is common. See CHARACTERS.

SQUIGGLE *(skwig':l)*. **SQIGGLE** *(skig':l) noun.*
The character " ~ " (tilde). Synonym: TWIDDLE.
   SQUIGGLE BRACKETS *noun.* The brace characters "{" and
"}".
See CHARACTERS.

STATE *noun.*
Condition, situation. Examples: "What's the state of your latest
hack?" "It's WINNING away." "The SYSTEM tried to read and
write the disk simultaneously and got into a totally WEDGED
state."
   A standard question is "What's your state?" which means
"What are you doing?" or "What are you about to do?" Typical
answers might be "I'm about to GRONK OUT" or "I'm hungry."
   Another standard question is "What's the state of the
world?" meaning "What's new?" or "What's going on?"

STOPPAGE *(stahp':j) noun.*
Extreme LOSSAGE resulting in something (usually vital) becoming completely unusable. Example: "The recent system stoppage was caused by a FRIED transformer."

SUPERPROGRAMMER *noun.*
A prolific programmer; one who can code exceedingly well and
quickly. Not all hackers are superprogrammers, but many are.
   Productivity can vary from one programmer to another by
factors of as much as 1000. For example, one programmer
might be able to write an average of 3 lines of working code
in one day, while another, with the proper tools and skill, might
be able to write 3000 lines of working code in one day. This
variance is astonishing, appearing in very few other areas of
human endeavor.
   Mark Crispin once reported, "While working at Stanford, I
wrote the first 96-bit leader PDP-10 Network Control Program
as my first monitor coding project. That took about two weeks,
and at the time nobody believed I had accomplished it because
someone on the East Coast had been working on it for over a
year and still hadn't finished. I understand I rocked some boats
when it was proven I had succeeded."

The term "superprogrammer" is more commonly used within such places as IBM than in the hacker community. It tends to stress productivity rather than creativity or ingenuity. Hackers prefer the terms HACKER and WIZARD.

SWAP *verb.*
1. To exchange; to trade places. See EXCH.
2. To move information from a fast-access memory to a slow-access memory (swap out), or vice versa (swap in). This is a technical term in computer science, and often specifically refers to the use of disks as "virtual memory." As pieces of data or program are needed, they are swapped into main memory for processing; when they are no longer needed for the nonce they are swapped out again. The slang use of these terms is as a fairly exact analogy referring to people's memories. Cramming for an exam might be spoken of as swapping in. If you temporarily forget someone's name but then remember it, your excuse is that it was swapped out. To "keep something swapped in" means to keep it fresh in your memory: "I reread the TECO manual every few months to keep it swapped in." If someone interrupts you just as you get a good idea, you might say, "Wait a moment while I write this down so I can swap it out," implying that if you don't write it down it will get swapped out (forgotten) as you talk.

SYSTEM *noun.*
1. The supervisor program on the computer; the program that is responsible for coordinating the activities of the various users of the computer.
2. The entire computer system, including input/output devices, the supervisor program, and possibly other software.
3. Any large-scale program.
4. Any method or methodology.
5. The way things are usually done.
6. The existing bureaucracy. "You can't beat the system."

SYSTEM HACKER *noun.* One who hacks the system (in sense 1 only; for sense 3 one mentions the particular program, as in LISP hacker or TECO hacker).

T *(tee)*

    1. A particular time. See TIME T. (The variable "T" is cus-
tomarily used in physics to represent points in or quantities
of time.)

    2. Yes. This word is used in reply to a question, particularly one
asked using the "-P" convention. Example: "Foodp?" "T."
That simple interchange means, "Do you want to come eat
with us?" "Sure." See NIL.

    In the LISP language, the name "T" means "true," among
other things. Some hackers use "T" and "NIL" instead of
"yes" and "no" almost reflexively. This sometimes causes
misunderstandings. When a waiter or flight attendant asks if
a hacker wants coffee, he may well respond "T," meaning
that he wants coffee; but of course he will be brought a cup
of tea instead. As it happens, most hackers like tea at least
as well as coffee—particularly those who frequent Chinese
restaurants—so it's not that big a problem.

TALK MODE

    A situation in which two or more terminals are logically linked
together so that whatever is typed on the keyboard of any one
appears on the screens of all. This is used for conversation via
computer. See COM MODE and MODE.

TASTE *noun.*

    1. Aesthetic pleasance; the quality in programs which tends to
be inversely proportional to the number of FEATURES,
HACKS, CROCKS, and KLUGES programmed into it.

    TASTY *adjective.* Aesthetically pleasing; FLAVORFUL. Exam-
ple: "This FEATURE comes in N tasty FLAVORS."

    Although "tasteful" and "flavorful" are essentially synonyms,
"taste" and "flavor" are not. "Taste" refers to sound judgment
on the part of the creator; a program or feature can *exhibit*
taste but cannot "have" taste. On the other hand, a feature can
have flavor. Also, "flavor" has the additional meaning of "kind"
or "variety" not shared by "taste." "Flavor" is a more popular
word among hackers than "taste", though both are used.

TECO *(tee'koh)*

    1. *noun.* A text editor developed at MIT and modified by just

about everybody. If all the dialects are included, TECO
might well be the single most prolific editor in use. Noted
for its powerful pseudo-programming features and its incredibly hairy syntax. As an example, here is a TECO program that takes a list of names like this . . .

Loser, J. Random
Quux, The Great
Dick, Moby

. . . sorts them alphabetically according to last name, and then
puts the last name last, removing the comma, to produce this:

Moby Dick
J. Random Loser
The Great Quux

The program is:

```
[1 J  ^  P $ L $ $
J <.-Z; .,(S,$ -D .)FX1 @F ^ B $K :L I $ Gl L> $$
```

In fact, this very program was used to produce the second,
sorted, list from the first list! The manuscript for this book was
produced using the EMACS editor, which is built on top of
TECO and allows you to execute TECO programs. The first
time I tried the program it had a BUG; I had accidentally omitted the "@" in front of "F ^ B", which, as anyone can see, is
clearly THE WRONG THING. It worked fine the second time.
There isn't space to describe all the features of TECO, but I will
note that " ^ P" means "sort" and "J <.-Z; . . . L>" is an
idiomatic series of commands for "do once for every line."
2. *verb.* To edit using the TECO editor in one of its infinite
    forms; sometimes used to mean "to edit" even when not
    using TECO!
    Mark Crispin provided these historical notes:

    Historical note (1): DEC grabbed an ancient version of MIT
TECO many years ago when it was still a TTY-oriented editor (that
is, didn't make use of display screens). By now, TECO at MIT is

highly display-oriented and is actually a programming language for writing editors such as EMACS, rather than being used as an editor itself. Meanwhile, the outside world's various versions of TECO remain almost the same as the MIT version of 1970 or so. DEC recently tried to discourage its use, but an underground movement of sorts kept it alive.

Historical note (2): Since note (1) was written, I found out that DEC tried to force their programmers by administrative decision to use a hacked-up and generally lobotomized version of SOS instead of TECO, and they revolted.

TENSE *adjective.*
Of programs, very clever and efficient. A tense piece of code often got that way because it was highly BUMMED, but sometimes it was just based on a great idea. As an example, this comment was found in a clever display routine by Mike Kazar, a student hacker at CMU: "This routine is so tense it will bring tears to your eyes. Much thanks to Craig Everhart and James Gosling for inspiring this HACK ATTACK."
A tense programmer is one who produces tense code. They say that PDP-10 code flows from the pencil of hacker Bill Gosper in a maximally tense state. I don't waste my time trying to bum even one instruction from a PDP-10 program if I learn that Gosper wrote it.

TENURED GRADUATE STUDENT *noun.*
One who has been in graduate school for ten years (the usual maximum is five or six): a "ten-yeared" student. (Get it?) Students don't really get tenure, of course, the way professors do, but a tenth-year graduate student has probably been around the university longer than any nontenured professor.

TERPRI *(tur'pree, t:r'pree) verb.*
To output a CRLF; to terminate a line of text and start the next line.
This comes from the name of the LISP routine that performs this action. It is a contraction of "TERminate PRInt line."

THEORY *noun.*
Any idea, plan, story, policy, or set of rules. This is a generaliza-

tion and abuse of the technical meaning. Examples: "What's the theory on fixing this TECO loss?" "What's the theory on dinner tonight?" ("Chinatown, I guess.") "What's the current theory on letting LOSERS on during the day?" "The theory behind this change is to fix the following well-known screw..."

THRASH *verb.*

To move wildly or violently without accomplishing anything useful. The connotation is of a maximum of motion with a minimum of effectiveness. Computer systems that are overloaded waste most of their time SWAPPING information between disk and memory rather than performing useful computation, and are therefore said to "thrash." Someone who keeps changing his mind is said to be thrashing.

TIME T *noun.*

A time or instant unspecified but understandable from context. Often used in conjunction with a later time, "$T+1$" or "$T+N$."

Example: "We'll meet on campus at time T or at Louie's at time T plus one" means, in the context of going out for dinner, "If we meet at Louie's directly, we can meet there a little later than if we meet on campus and then have to travel to Louie's." (Louie's is a Chinese restaurant in Palo Alto that is a favorite with hackers. Louie makes the best potstickers I've ever tasted. See RAV.) Had "thirty" been used instead of "one," it would have implied that the travel time from campus to Louie's is thirty minutes. Whatever time "T" is (and that hasn't been decided yet), you can meet half an hour later at Louie's than you could on campus and end up eating at the same time.

SINCE (OR AT) TIME T EQUALS MINUS INFINITY. A long time ago; for as long as anyone can remember; at the time that some particular FROB was first designed. "That feature has been BROKEN since time T equals minus infinity."

Sometimes the word "time" is omitted if there is no danger of confusing T as a time with T meaning "yes." See T.

TOGGLE *verb.*

To change a BIT from whatever state it is in to the other state:

to change from 1 to 0 or from 0 to 1. This probably comes from "toggle switches," such as standard light switches—though the word *toggle* apparently originally referred to the mechanism that keeps the switch in the position to which it is flipped, rather than to the fact that the switch has two positions.

There are four things you can do to a bit: set it (force it to be 1), clear (or zero) it, leave it alone, or toggle it. (Mathematically, one would say that there are four distinct boolean-valued functions of one boolean argument, but saying that is *much* less fun than talking about toggling bits.)

TOOL

1. *verb.* To work hard; to study; to "cram" for an exam. This is an antonym of sorts for HACK: "tooling" is working without enjoying it. The distinction is useful to hackers who are also students: tooling is programming or other work done for courses. Example: "I have to tool chemistry for a while before I GRONK OUT."

2. *noun.* A person who (seemingly) always tools and never hacks; a nerd (or nurd). This term is used throughout MIT. Students refer to themselves with more or less pride as "Tech tools."

TRASH-80 *noun.*

A Radio Shack TRS-80 personal computer.

Hackers are accustomed to using powerful, million-dollar computers, and tend to look down a little on itty-bitty computers that can't deliver enough CYCLES for their purposes. This is not to say that personal computers can't be useful, or that some hackers don't enjoy working with them. Personal computers are getting better all the time. Observe, however, that many programs being sold for personal computers are developed on much larger computers that provide a better programming environment.

The name "Trash-80" is used more as a play on the name of the product than as a judgment on the product as compared to its competitors. The term is used in good spirit by TRS-80 owners as well.

TTY *(tit'ee) noun.*
  1. A computer terminal of the Teletype variety, characterized
     by a noisy mechanical printer, a very limited character set,
     and poor print quality. This term is antiquated (like the
     TTYs themselves). The definition must be considered rela-
     tive to modern terminals. In their heyday, TTYs were useful
     and fairly reliable workhorses.
  2. Any computer terminal at all, especially the one that is con-
     trolling a computer program under discussion, or that the
     program can display information on. Example: "This pro-
     gram lists the current file directory on the TTY."
        See also GLASS TTY.

TWEAK *verb.*
  To change slightly, relative to some reference point; to adjust
  finely. If a program is almost correct, rather than figuring out
  the precise problem you might just keep tweaking it until it
  works.
     Synonym: TWIDDLE. See also FROBNICATE and FUDGE FAC-
  TOR.

TWENEX *(twen'eks) noun.*
  The TOPS-20 operating system distributed by DEC for the
  DECSYSTEM-20 computer, a successor to the PDP-10. There
  was an operating system for the PDP-10 called TOPS-10, so
  TOPS-20 is an obvious name for a DECSYSTEM-20 operating
  system, even though TOPS-20 is nothing like TOPS-10. TOPS-
  10 was a typically CRUFTY operating system produced by DEC
  itself. The firm of Bolt, Beranek, and Newman (BBN) developed its own operating system, called TENEX (for "TEN EX-
  ecutive system"). DEC obtained the right to use TENEX and
  extended it to create TOPS-20. The term "TWENEX" is therefore a contraction of "twenty TENEX." DEC people tend to
  cringe when they hear TOPS-20 referred to as "TWENEX,"
  but the term seems to be catching on nevertheless. The abbreviation "20x" is also used and also pronounced "TWENEX."

TWIDDLE *(twid':l)*
  1. *noun.* The tilde character " ~ ". See CHARACTERS.

2. *noun.* A small and insignificant change to a program. A twiddle usually fixes one BUG and generates several new ones.
3. *verb.* To change something in a small way. BITS, for example, are often twiddled. Twiddling a switch or knob implies much less sense of purpose than TOGGLING or TWEAKING it: see FROBNICATE. To speak of twiddling a bit connotes aimlessness, and at best doesn't specify what you're doing to the bit; by contrast, toggling a bit has a more specific meaning.

UP *adjective.*
Working; in order. Example: "The Down escalator is up." Antonym: DOWN.

BRING UP *verb.* To create a working version and start it. Examples: "They just brought up the system." "JONL is going to bring up a new LISP compiler tonight." Antonym: TAKE DOWN.

USER *noun.*
1. Someone doing "real work" with the computer, who uses a computer as a means rather than an end. Someone who pays to use a computer. See REAL USER.
2. A programmer who will believe anything you tell him. One who asks silly questions. See LUSER.
3. Someone who uses a program from the outside, however skillfully, without getting into the internals of the program. One who reports BUGS instead of just going ahead and fixing them.

Basically, there are two classes of people who work with a program: there are implementors (HACKERS) and users (LOSERS). The users are looked down on by hackers to a mild degree because they don't understand the full ramifications of the SYSTEM in all its glory. (The few users who do are known as REAL WINNERS.)

The term is a relative one: A consummate hacker may be a user with respect to some program he himself does not hack. A LISP hacker might be one who maintains LISP or one who uses LISP (but with the skill of a hacker). A LISP user is one who uses LISP, whether skillfully or not. Thus there is some overlap between the two terms; the subtle distinctions must be resolved by context.

It is true that users ask questions (of necessity). Sometimes they are thoughtful or deep. Very often they are annoying or downright stupid, apparently because the user failed to think for two seconds or to look in the documentation before bothering the maintainer.

VANILLA *adjective.*

Standard, usual, of ordinary FLAVOR. "It's just a vanilla terminal; it doesn't have any interesting FEATURES."

When used of food, this term very often does not mean that the food is flavored with vanilla extract! For example, "vanilla-flavored wonton soup" (or simply "vanilla wonton soup") means ordinary wonton soup, as opposed to hot-and-sour wonton soup.

This word differs from CANONICAL in that the latter means "the thing you always use (or the way you always do it) unless you have some strong reason to do otherwise," whereas "vanilla" simply means "ordinary." For example, when MIT hackers go to Colleen's Chinese Cuisine, hot-and-sour wonton soup is the *canonical* wonton soup to get (because that is what most of them usually order) even though it isn't the *vanilla* wonton soup.

VAXEN *(vaks':n)*

The plural usually used among hackers for the DEC VAX computers. "Our installation has four PDP-10's and twenty vaxen."

The DEC operating system for the VAX is called VMS (for Virtual Memory System). It has its advantages, but sometimes it seems to run rather slowly. Hence this limerick:

There once was a system called VMS
Of cycles by no means abstemious.
    It's chock-full of hacks
    And runs on a VAX
And makes my poor stomach all squeamious.

–The Great QUUX

VIRTUAL *adjective.*

Performing the functions of. Virtual memory acts like real memory but isn't. (A virtual memory system uses a combination of a small main memory plus a magnetic disk to give the illusion that a computer has a large main memory. It does this by SWAPPING information between the main memory and the disk as needed.)

This term is synonymous with LOGICAL, except that "virtual" is never used with compass directions.

VISIONARY *noun.*

One who HACKS vision, in the sense of an artificial intelligence researcher working on the problem of getting computers to "see" things using TV cameras. (There isn't any problem in sending information from a TV camera to a computer. The problem is, how can the computer be programmed to make use of the camera information? See SMOP.)

WALL *interjection.*

An indication of confusion, usually spoken with a quizzical tone. "Wall?" A request for further explication.

This seems to be a shortened form of "Hello, wall," apparently from the phrase "up against a blank wall." This term is used primarily at WPI.

WALLPAPER *noun.*

A program listing or, especially, a transcript of all or part of a login session, showing everything that ever appeared on the terminal. (The idea was that the LPT paper for such listings was essentially good only for wallpaper, as evidenced at Stanford where it was in fact used as wallpaper to cover windows to keep the light out.)

WALLPAPER FILE *noun.* The file that contains the wallpaper information before it is actually printed on paper. (Sometimes you don't intend ever to produce a real paper copy of the file, because you can look at the file directly on your terminal, but it is still called a "wallpaper file.")

This term is used infrequently nowadays, especially since

other SYSTEMS have developed other terms for the concept (for example: PHOTO on TWENEX). The term possibly originated on the ITS system at MIT, where the commands to begin and end transcript files are still ":WALBEG" and ":WALEND", which produce a file named "WALL PAPER."

WEDGED *adjective*.
1. To be stuck, incapable of proceeding without help. This is different from having CRASHED. If the system has crashed, then it has become totally nonfunctioning. If the system is "wedged," it is trying to do something but cannot make progress. It may be capable of doing a few things, but not be fully operational. For example, the system may become wedged if the disk controller FRIES; there are some things you can do without using the disks, but not many. Being wedged is slightly milder than being "hung." This term is sometimes used as a synonym for DEADLOCKED. See also HANG, LOSING, CATATONIA, and BUZZ.
2. Of a person, suffering severely from misconceptions. Examples: "He's totally wedged—he's convinced that he can levitate through meditation." "I'm sorry. I had a BIT set that you were responsible for TECO, but I was wedged."

   WEDGITUDE *(wedj'i-tood)*. The quality or state of being wedged.

WHEEL *noun*.
1. A "privilege" BIT that, when set, CANONICALLY allows the possessor to perform any operation whatsoever on a time-sharing system, such as read or write any file on the system regardless of protections, change or look at any address in the running monitor, CRASH or reload the SYSTEM, and kill or create jobs and USER accounts. The term was invented on the TENEX operating system and carried over to TOPS-20 and others. See TWENEX.
2. A person who possesses a set wheel bit (and who therefore has great privilege and power on that system). "We need to find a wheel to unwedge the hung tape drives."

   WHEEL WARS. A period during which student wheels HACK

each other by attempting to log each other out of the system, delete each other's files, or otherwise wreak havoc—usually at the expense of the lesser USERS.

WIN

1. *verb.* To succeed. A program wins if no unexpected conditions arise. Antonym: LOSE.
2. *noun.* Success, or a specific instance thereof. A pleasing outcome. A FEATURE. Emphatic forms: MOBY win, super win, hyper-win. For some reason "suitable win" is also common at MIT, usually in reference to a satisfactory solution to a problem. Antonym: LOSS.

BIG WIN *noun.* The results of serendipity.

WIN BIG *verb.* To experience serendipity. "I went shopping and won big; there was a two-for-one sale."

WIN, WIN *interjection.*

WINNER *noun.* An unexpectedly good situation, program, programmer, or person. Albert Einstein was a winner. Antonym: LOSER.

REAL WINNER *noun.* This term is often used sarcastically, but is also used as high praise.

WINNAGE *(win'-j) noun.* The situation when a LOSSAGE is corrected or when something is winning. Quite rare. Usage: also quite rare.

WINNITUDE *(win'-tood) noun.* The quality of winning (as opposed to WINNAGE, which is the result of winning).

WIZARD *noun.*

1. A person who knows how a complex piece of software or hardware works (that is, who GROKS it); someone who can find and fix BUGS quickly in an emergency. This term differs somewhat from HACKER. Someone is a hacker if he has general hacking ability, but is only a wizard with respect to something if he has specific, detailed knowledge of that thing. A good hacker could become a wizard of something, given the time to study it.
2. A person who is permitted to do things forbidden to ordinary people. For example, an Adventure wizard at Stanford may play the Adventure game during the day, which is

forbidden (the program simply refuses to play) to most people because it uselessly consumes too many CYCLES.

WIZARDLY *adjective.* Pertaining to wizards. A wizardly FEATURE is one that only a wizard could understand or use properly.

WOW

The exclamation point character "!". Synonyms: BANG, EXCL, SHRIEK.

See CHARACTERS.

WRONG THING, THE *noun.*

The opposite of THE RIGHT THING; more generally, anything that is not the right thing. In cases where "the good is the enemy of the best," the merely good, while good, is nevertheless the wrong thing.

XOR *(eks'ohr) conjunction.*

Exclusive or. "A xor B" means "A or B, but definitely not both." Example: "I want to get cherry pie xor a banana split." This derives from the technical use of the term as a function on truth-values that is true if either of two arguments is true but not both.

XYZZY *(eks'wie'zee'zee'wie, zi'zee)*

The CANONICAL "magic word." This comes from the Adventure game, in which the idea is to explore an underground cave with many rooms to collect treasure. If you type XYZZY at the appropriate time, you can move instantly between two otherwise distant points.

If, therefore, you encounter some bit of MAGIC, or more precisely some technique for accomplishing magic, you might remark on this quite succinctly by saying simply "XYZZY!" This may be translated roughly as "Wow! Magic!" Example: "Ordinarily you can't look at someone else's screen if he has protected it, but if you type quadruple-bucky-CLEAR the system will let you do it anyway." "XYZZY!"

YOYO MODE *noun.*

A state in which the system is said to be when it rapidly alternates several times between being UP and being DOWN.

YU-SHIANG WHOLE FISH *(yoo'hsyang', yoo'shang')* *noun.*
The Greek letter lower-case gamma when written with a loop
in its tail "ɣ", making it look like a little fish swimming down
the page. The term is actually the name of a Chinese dish in
which a fish is cooked whole (not PARSED) and covered with Yu
Shiang sauce. This bit of slang is used primarily by people on
the MIT LISP Machine computers, which can display this character on their screens. The term also tends to elicit incredulity
from people who hear about it secondhand. See CHARACTERS.

ZAP
1. *noun.* Spiciness.
2. *verb.* To make food spicy.
3. *verb.* To make someone "suffer" by making his food spicy.
   (Most hackers love spicy food. Hot-and-sour soup is wimpy
   unless it makes you blow your nose for the rest of the meal.)
   ZAPPED *adjective.* Of food, spicy. "Watch out—that bean
curd dish is really zapped tonight." Of people, wiped out or
GRONKED because of eating spicy food. "I ate the bean curd
and got totally zapped. I used up two boxes of Kleenex. It was
great."
   This term is used to distinguish between food that is hot (in
temperature) and food that is "hot," that is, spicy. For example,
the Chinese appetizer Bon Bon Chicken is a kind of chicken
salad that is cold but zapped.
   Hacker Bill Gosper has one of the highest tolerances for
zapped food. He frequently eats at Louie's, a Chinese restaurant in Palo Alto (actually called "Hsi Nan," but hackers who
know the owner refer to it simply as Louie's); and Louie will
frequently try to out-zap him. When he does, you don't want
to get caught in the cross fire. The food is absolutely delicious,
but you would think that the sauce contains nitric acid.

ZERO *verb.*
1. To set to zero. Usually said of small pieces of data such as
   BITS or words.
2. By extension, to erase; to discard all data from. Said of disks

and directories, where "zeroing" need not involve actually writing zeroes throughout the area being zeroed. One may speak of something being LOGICALLY zeroed (forgotten) rather than being physically zeroed (erased).

ZORCH *(zohrch)*

1. *verb.* To move quickly, like a rocket ship trailing fire behind it. "This file transfer program is very fast; it really zorches those files through the network."

2. *noun.* Influence, "brownie points"; that intangible and fuzzy currency in which favors are measured. "I'd rather not ask him for that just yet; I think I've used up my quota of zorch with him for the week."

3. *noun.* Energy or ability. "I guess I'll PUNT fixing that bug until tomorrow. I've been up for thirty hours and I've run out of zorch."

About the Authors

GLS *(gliss)* **Guy L. Steele Jr.**
I earned my A.B. degree (1975) in applied mathematics at Harvard College, and my S.M. (1977) and Ph.D. (1980) degrees in computer science and artificial intelligence at MIT. Since 1980 I have been an assistant professor of computer science at Carnegie-Mellon University, now on leave. Now I am a Senior Scientist at Tartan Laboratories, Incorporated. I have been hacking computers for fifteen years. I am married to another hacker, Barbara K. Steele, and we have two children. I enjoy cooking Chinese food, doing carpentry, cartooning, singing, and playing piano and guitar. But for real fun, nothing can beat an all-night hack session, preferably writing hairy TECO code for EMACS.
Synonym: QUUX.

DON *(dahn)* **Donald R. Woods.**
My father got me interested in computers at the age of 11, back when that was still unusual. One of my very first hacks earned me $50 when his company decided to use it as a demonstration at one of the trade fairs. I studied electrical engineering at Princeton (B.S.E., 1975), mainly because they didn't have an undergraduate computer science program. Then I came out to Stanford where, after the obligatory dawdling and hacking, I contrived to earn a Ph.D. (1981) in computer science. By that time I was working for the Xerox Corporation, and I've been there ever since. Besides contributing to the "jargon file," I'm probably best known as coauthor (with Jim Lyon) of the INTERCAL Programming Language Reference Manual, and as one of the primary authors of the original Adventure program.

RF *(ahr'eff)* **Raphael A. Finkel.**
I received an A.B. degree in mathematics and an M.A.T. degree in teaching from the University of Chicago in 1972, and in 1976 a Ph.D. degree in computer science from Stanford University. I am now an associate professor in the Department of Computer Sciences, University of Wisconsin, Madison. Teaching is important to me, and I have received two teaching awards: the Sperry Univac 1979–1980 Computer Science Professor of the Year Award, and a 1981 University Distinguished Teaching Award. My research is in the general area of distributed algorithms; in particular, I have built several distributed operating systems. Outside of work, I enjoy studying Judaica (Mishna, Gemorra, and Yiddish) and playing piano. I don't hack much any more.

MRC *(murk, m:rk)* **Mark R. Crispin.**
I earned my B.S. degree (1977) in Technology and Society at Stevens Institute of Technology. Since graduating I have been a systems programmer at the Computer Science Department at Stanford University. I'm married to hacker and aspiring broadcasting personality Lynn Ann Gold; my BMW 320i's license plate is California ILVLYNN. Besides hacking, we ice skate, ski, go to punk rock concerts, collect science fiction artwork, and are dragon lovers and ardent bad movie fanatics. One recent thrill was seeing *Plan Nine from Outer Space,* winner of the Golden Turkey award as the "worst movie ever made" (I agree with that assessment). We have several home computers, one of which runs an X-rated electronic bulletin-board system popular with many of the perverts in the San Francisco Bay Area.

RMS *(ahr'em'ess')* **Richard M. Stallman.**
I was built at a laboratory in Manhattan around 1953, and moved to the MIT Artificial Intelligence Lab in 1971. My hobbies include affection, international folk dance, flying, cooking, physics, recorder, puns, science fiction fandom, and programming; I magically get paid for doing the last one. About a year ago I split up with the PDP-10 computer to which I was married for ten years. We still love each other, but the world is

taking us in different directions. For the moment I still live in Cambridge, Massachusetts, among our old memories. "Richard Stallman" is just my mundane name; you can call me "RMS."

GFF *(jef)* **Geoffrey S. Goodfellow.**
I've been a hacker ever since I ran into a model-33 TTY connected at the lightning speed of 110 bps between my seventh grade school and a PDP-10 running TENEX at Stanford University. Since my introduction to the world of hacking, formal education has held no allure for me. Two weeks into the final quarter of my senior year of high school, I dropped out and accepted a job at SRI International in Menlo Park, California. I have not returned to class since I flushed school and have no degree of any type to my name. Today, my most productive hacking is accompished at my residence where I'm connected up to an ersatz PDP-10, a Foonly-F4, running TENEX in SRI's computer science lab via a 9600 bps leased line. Professionally, my interests are primarily computer packet-switched networks, security, office automation, electronic mail, cellular radio, and mobile communications. Nonprofessionally, I like to hack, travel, eat out at fine restaurants, collect cars, and watch an occasional movie on my 6-foot projection TV.